Helping Children to Build Self-Esteem

also by Deborah Plummer

Self-Esteem Games for Children
Illustrations by Jane Serrurier
ISBN 978 1 84310 424 7

The Adventures of the Little Tin Tortoise
A Self-Esteem Story with Activities for Teachers, Parents and Carers
Illustrations by Jane Serrurier
ISBN 978 1 84310 406 3

Helping Adolescents and Adults to Build Self-Esteem
A Photocopiable Resource Book
ISBN 978 1 84310 185 7

Using Interactive Imagework with Children
Walking on the Magic Mountain
ISBN 978 1 85302 671 3

of related interest

Special Stories for Disability Awareness
Stories and Activities for Teachers, Parents and Professionals
Mal Leicester
Illustrations by Taryn Shrigley-Wightman
ISBN 978 1 84310 390 5

Chasing Ideas
The Fun of Freeing Your Child's Imagination
Revised Edition
Christine Durham
ISBN 978 1 84310 460 5

Working with Anger and Young People
Nick Luxmoore
ISBN 978 1 84310 466 7

Classroom Tales
Using Storytelling to Build Emotional, Social and Academic Skills
across the Primary Curriculum
Jennifer M. Fox Eades
ISBN 978 1 84310 304 2

A Safe Place for Caleb
An Interactive Book for Kids, Teens, and Adults with Issues of Attachment,
Grief and Loss, or Early Trauma
Kathleen A. Chara and Paul J. Chara, Jr.
ISBN 978 1 84310 799 6

Emotional Healing and Self-Esteem
Inner-life Skills of Relaxation, Visualisation and Meditation
for Children and Adolescents
Mark Pearson
ISBN 978 1 84310 224 3

Helping Children to Build Self-Esteem

A Photocopiable Activities Book

Second Edition

Deborah M. Plummer

Illustrations by Alice Harper

Jessica Kingsley Publishers
London and Philadelphia

First edition published in 2001

This edition published in 2007
by Jessica Kingsley Publishers
116 Pentonville Road
London N1 9JB, UK
and
400 Market Street, Suite 400
Philadelphia, PA 19106, USA

www.jkp.com

Library of Congress Cataloging in Publication Data
Plummer, Deborah.
 Helping children to build self-esteem : a photocopiable activities book / Deborah M. Plummer ; illustrations by Alice Harper. -- 2nd ed.
   p. cm.
 Includes bibliographical references and index.
 ISBN 978-1-84310-488-9 (pbk.)
 1. Self-esteem in children. I. Title.
 BF723.S3P58 2007
 155.4'182--dc22
                         2006037059

British Library Cataloguing in Publication Data
A CIP catalogue record for this book is available from the British Library

ISBN 978 1 84310 488 9

Printed and Bound in the United States by Thomson-Shore, Inc.

Contents

Part Four   Working with Parents

Acknowledgements

Some of the ideas presented here may be familiar to you, as they are based on well-established strategies for promoting self-esteem. However, most have 'developed themselves' either on the spot during therapy or during the preparation and debriefing periods for some of the many children's groups and parent workshops I have facilitated as a speech and language therapist.

My main source of inspiration has been imagework, for which I have Dina Glouberman to thank. Her creative and unique courses, her ongoing support and the support of my fellow imagework practitioners have all been nothing less than magical!

My grateful thanks go to all the children who have tried out these exercises so enthusiastically, to all the parents who have taught me so much (particularly about the realities of trying to fit 'homework' tasks into a busy family schedule!) and to my niece Alice Harper, who patiently redrew all the illustrations for this edition just days before flying off to work in an orphanage in Nepal.

Finally, my thanks to the team at Jessica Kingsley Publishers, particularly commissioning editor Stephen Jones and project editor Lyndsey Dodd.

Introduction

This is the second edition of what essentially remains a practical resource for helping young children to explore their imaginative abilities and enhance their self-esteem. The theoretical section, although updated and expanded, therefore remains relatively short, providing a framework for the activities and a basis for practitioners who would like to investigate any of these aspects in more depth. Parts Two and Three of the book are devoted to the application of the ideas. The basic format for these sections is unchanged but there are substantial additions to Part Two (Instructions for Self-Esteem Activities) and some alterations to the activity sheets. The activities are child-centred and are based on a combination of therapeutic approaches, in particular imagework (see Chapter 1) and personal construct psychology (e.g. Kelly 1991).

The photocopiable handouts are suitable for children aged 7–11 years and can be used either as a complete course or as a resource to dip into and adapt as needed. This allows for flexibility in how the material is used, enabling therapists, teachers, social workers, counsellors, nurses, psychologists and other professionals to utilise the handouts and activity ideas with individuals and groups in a variety of settings. In my own work I have used the ideas presented here with children who stutter, children who have mild language impairments and children who have no specific speech or language difficulties but who are underachieving at school or have poor social skills.

I have also used many of the ideas in an adapted format for slightly older children. Instead of using the concept of collecting treasure as they complete the worksheets, they are encouraged to view these activities as steps to discovering and developing their 'life skills'. Similarly, instead of using magic and magicians, we talk in terms of the power of their own minds and the sense of control and self-direction they can achieve through understanding the way that they think and how this affects their feelings and actions. The principle remains the same for all ages: active use of the imagination promotes a fuller understanding of self and encourages realistic self-evaluation, creative problem-solving and realistic goal-setting.

Since the first edition of this book was published in 2001 I have been fortunate in being invited to run workshops for a wide variety of students and professionals. Groups as diverse as therapeutic social workers, family support workers, teachers, speech and language therapists and police officers working with vulnerable witnesses, have all confirmed just how central the issues of self-esteem are seen to be by those who work with children.

Such discussions have also led to the inclusion of a 'working with parents' section in this edition (Part Four). The influence of important adults is obviously a major factor in the building and maintenance of healthy self-esteem in children. We are not born with self-esteem, it is something which develops over time, with its roots in babyhood and its establishment intimately connected with our early experiences. Part Four of this book therefore offers a suggested format for introducing parents to ways of supporting emergent self-esteem or helping children to build self-esteem where there is already an identified difficulty.

Please note that throughout the text when referring to 'a child' the pronouns 'he' and 'she' have been used interchangeably.

Reference

Kelly, G.A. (1991) *The Psychology of Personal Constructs, Vol 1: A Theory of Personality.* London: Routledge, in association with the Centre for Personal Construct Psychology.

Suggestions for further reading

Dalton, P. and Dunnett, G. (1992) *A Psychology for Living: Personal Construct Theory for Professionals and Clients.* Chichester: Wiley.

Fransella, F. and Dalton, P. (1990) *Personal Construct Counselling in Action.* London: Sage.

Glouberman, D. (2003) *Life Choices, Life Changes: Develop Your Personal Vision with Imagework* (revised edition). London: Hodder and Stoughton.

Part One

Theoretical Background

Chapter 1

Imagery, Imagework and the Process of Change

This chapter offers a brief explanation of imagework and explores the idea of helping children to utilise their natural imaginative abilities to create positive future choices.

What are images?

Images of one sort or another are a natural part of our lives and are our earliest means of making sense of the world. They form the basis of our knowledge about ourselves and others and about our environment long before we are ever able to communicate through words.

> Many of our guiding images emerge in infancy and early childhood, at a time when imagery is the dominant mode of thought, and they guide not only our thoughts but our body functioning and our whole way of being. (Glouberman 2003, p.44)

Throughout life we build up a memory bank of images; one which reflects our uniquely personal *interpretations* of our experiences and interactions. While many of these images may be recalled fairly easily, there are countless others which pass into our unconscious minds, stored away in the 'vaults' and yet still capable of informing our daily lives. Sometimes they influence us to such an extent that we may feel as though we have little choice about our feelings, attitudes or actions. Indeed, Carl Jung went so far as to describe the unconscious as 'a living psychic entity which, it seems, is relatively autonomous, behaving as if it were a personality with intentions of its own' (Jung 1990, p.17).

However, he also depicted the unconscious as being far more than just a depository of the past:

> Completely new thoughts and creative ideas can present themselves from the unconscious – thoughts that have never been conscious before. They grow up from the dark depths of the mind like a lotus and form a most important part of the subliminal psyche. (Jung 1978, p.25)

The exploration of personal imagery is the basis of many forms of therapy and counselling, since being more aware of how our images affect our thinking and behaviour can help us to make more informed choices in life. The richness and creativity of the unconscious mind also means that it is possible for us to create new images. These can replace or outweigh those formed through past experiences which are no longer useful for our self-development. This latter aspect is the foundation for the imagework in this book.

What is imagework?

The term 'imagework' was created by Dr Dina Glouberman to describe a particular way of working with imagery, but the idea of interacting with personal images is not new, of course. The process is centuries old and played an important part in the healing traditions of many ancient cultures.

In the nineteenth century Jung developed the idea of 'active imagination' and encouraged his patients to use it as a self-help tool. Active imagination starts from the premise that the unconscious has its own wisdom so, although the person is participating fully in the process, she allows her imagination to flow where it wants and then works with whatever images arise. The imagination then acts as a 'meeting place' between the conscious and the unconscious mind, a 'common ground where both meet on equal terms and together create a life experience that combines the elements of both' (Johnson 1989, p.140). Johnson suggests that by talking to images and interacting with them in this way in our imagination we will invariably find that 'they tell you things you never consciously knew and express thoughts that you never consciously thought' (Johnson 1989, p.138).

James Hillman advises us to remember that images do not require interpretation (see, for example, 'Imaginal Practice' in Moore 1990). He suggests that we do not need to interpret the images that arise but that the image itself is more important, more inclusive and more complex than what we have to say about it. We need the image, not the explanation, to help us on our path.

In other words, images demand respect not analysis! It is important to remember this when helping children to use their imagination. We can encourage them to talk about their images and to talk *with* their images but we should resist any temptation to offer our own interpretations as to what they might mean. Images are generally very personal to the individual. They should be seen in the context of where, when and how they were created, and in the light of each child's way of viewing the world.

This element of uniqueness in images means that both stored and newly created images come in many forms. Some people can see things clearly in their imagination; others may have a 'sense' of an image rather than a clear picture. Some people have mostly auditory images; others have mostly kinaesthetic (sensation) images. There is no right or wrong way of perceiving an image and even if two people have the same image they may *experience* it very differently.

Imagework and self-esteem

Children with low self-esteem appear to have very strong patternings of negative images. As I have suggested elsewhere (Plummer 2007) this image patterning contributes to (or perhaps formulates) the 'story' that they tell themselves about who they are.

For example, an image that a child might have of herself failing in one situation interconnects with a myriad other images until she eventually sees herself as 'a person who fails'. In this instance part of her story might be: 'I'm rubbish; I can't do anything as well as the rest of the class. Nobody wants to be friends with me. Everyone thinks I'm stupid...' These images of a 'rubbish', useless person whom nobody likes will inform the way that this child feels, learns and relates to others, not just at the moment of telling herself the story but also in the future, because if she tells the story often enough the images will be imprinted in her unconscious. In this way, even if she has concepts of herself which are not consistent with reality, they are true for her because she *believes* them to be true at a very deep level.

Tragically, many children originally hear and sense such stories from important adults in their lives; this builds and reinforces these negative image patterns from their babyhood and profoundly affects their emergent sense of self from the very start of life.

Imaginative reconstruing

Is it possible to help a child to alter this negative image patterning? Thankfully, yes, although it will take some creativity on our part as well as a sensitive acceptance of where the child is starting from, and it will be undeniably difficult if her life experiences have been consistently damaging. We should also be aware that there may be a marked time lag before the way that she interacts with others 'catches up' with the new version of her internal story. (Although in some instances, the reverse may be true – a child may learn to behave in certain ways in order to cover up her true sense of low self-worth so that it is the feelings which have to catch up with the behaviour.)

This means that we cannot always rely on observable behaviour alone to give an indication of levels of self-esteem (see p.229–230 and Appendix A). It also points to the fact that adults need to be aware of their vital role in helping children not only to *develop* self-esteem but also to *maintain* healthy self-esteem in the midst of life's challenges and inconsistencies.

There are many approaches to helping children to work with their images in a constructive way. I originally began by using images in the framework of guided journeys or stories, encouraging children to interact with the characters and objects that they met and to create their own images to represent problems, dilemmas and questions (Plummer 1999). It soon became evident that many of the children with whom I worked in this way also benefited from using shorter imagery exercises and expansion activities to facilitate the transition from internalised images to the practical applications of skills in everyday life (the basis of the activities in this book).

Of course, we can also help children to change their outward behaviour (as in behavioural therapy) or we can help them to change the story that they are telling themselves (cognitive therapy). But whichever approach we use, changes in one dimension are bound to have repercussions in the others – it is not possible to change one aspect alone without influencing the others since they are all intimately connected. So, for example, when a child changes the story that she tells herself, she gradually changes the unconscious images that inform her behaviour and she will begin to act in ways that are congruent with her new thoughts and beliefs.

By providing children with the means to foster creative use of their imaginations we can help them to build a unified sense of their inner and outer worlds; help them to see events, problems and challenges from a different viewpoint and enable them to find the way forward that is most appropriate for their individual needs. The resultant ability to make more informed choices in life will surely lead to a feeling of control, and will contribute to healthy levels of self-esteem, more effective learning and more fulfilling relationships.

If you decide to follow this route with an individual child or a group of children then I am sure that you will find that the strategies become second nature and you will soon be encouraging children to 'image' problems, decisions, dilemmas and feelings. You can also *offer* images if it seems appropriate – 'When you were really angry with Sam just now, I got this image of a tiger that had been hurt. Is that how you felt?' or 'This problem seems like a huge lump of rock to me – we just can't seem to shift it. What could we do about this rock?' Children who are used to this way of exploring images are often more than willing to put you right and to suggest their own images if they think you haven't quite grasped the essence of what they are feeling: 'No, it's more like a big swampy puddle...!' Simply talking about images in this way can often enable a child to see solutions or can precipitate a shift in perception where none seemed possible before.

References

Glouberman, D. (2003) *Life Choices, Life Changes: Develop Your Personal Vision with Imagework* (revised edition). London: Hodder and Stoughton.

Johnson, R. (1989) *Inner Work: Using Dreams and Active Imagination for Personal Growth*. New York: HarperSanFrancisco.

Jung, C.G. (ed.) (1978) *Man and His Symbols*. London: Pan Books.

Jung, C.G. (1990) Foreword in E. Neumann *Depth Psychology and a New Ethic*. Boston and Shaftesbury: Shambhala. (Original work published 1949.)

Moore, T. (ed.) (1990) *The Essential James Hillman: A Blue Fire*. London: Routledge.

Plummer, D. (1999) *Using Interactive Imagework with Children: Walking on the Magic Mountain.* London: Jessica Kingsley Publishers.

Plummer, D. (2007) *Self-Esteem Games for Children.* London: Jessica Kingsley Publishers.

Suggestions for further reading

Bettelheim, B. (1978) *The Uses of Enchantment.* Harmondsworth: Penguin.

Tyrrell, J. (2001) *The Power of Fantasy in Early Learning.* London and New York: Routledge.

Chapter 2

Understanding Self-Esteem

This chapter outlines some of the current knowledge about the origins of self-esteem, the concept of multi-dimensional models of self-esteem and various implications of the research findings.

As with any intervention strategies, the activities in this book will be most effective if facilitators have knowledge of these theories. This enables creative adjustments to be made to the materials according to the needs of individuals and groups while still working within a recognised framework. Supporting children in building self-esteem then becomes an 'attitude and an approach' (Gurney 1988, p.126); it is a way of being rather than a procedure with an end product or something we do to children to 'make them feel better'.

What is self-esteem? How do we measure it? How does it develop? What happens when self-esteem is low? These questions have been addressed in numerous research articles, academic textbooks and self-help books over the last 20 years or so, reflecting the widespread recognition that self-esteem is a primary factor in the building and maintenance of social, emotional and mental well-being and that it also plays a major part in academic achievements and physical health.

The quality of early infant–parent bonding and the formation of secure attachments have long been recognised as major factors in the development of a healthy self-concept and feelings of self-worth and competency (e.g. Ainsworth, Bell and Stayton 1971; Bowlby 1969; Main and Solomon 1990). Patterns of self-esteem established in early childhood perpetuate through adolescence and into adulthood and have far-reaching effects not only on the individual but on family groups and on wider society. We might speculate on the essence of 'family esteem' and 'cultural esteem', but the roots of these concepts must surely lie in the imperative for nurturing healthy self-esteem in young children. This in turn will involve supporting parents and carers, especially those who are struggling with their own issues regarding self-worth and competency.

I use the term 'healthy self-esteem' in recognition of the fact that we need to take into account family and cultural perspectives and that 'high self-esteem' may sometimes (wrongly) be seen as based almost entirely on feeling good about oneself, possibly to the detriment of others. This is not, of course, what we are aiming for when we set out to support the development and maintenance of healthy self-esteem. In fact, it could be argued that many children and adults who show some of the features associated with being self-absorbed or arrogant actually have low self-esteem and are therefore over-compensating in their attempts to feel better about themselves.

The ups and downs of the self-esteem debate have been written about extensively (e.g. Mruk 1999) but one thing remains certain: the term 'self-esteem' is now well established in our everyday language. Low self-esteem is frequently the topic of articles in parenting magazines and popular psychology books; it is an area of concern for many parents whose children are struggling socially or academically and it will crop up time and time again in therapeutic environments and in schools.

My experience has been that self-esteem is often viewed by parents, carers and many adult clients as a hard-to-capture resource rather than something that can be nurtured through loving, mindful interactions and through building specific skills and knowledge. This situation is gradually changing, however. Now, armed with more knowledge about self-esteem, we are in a better position to support its healthy growth and maintenance and to incorporate well-researched principles into our daily interactions with children.

The neuroscience of self-esteem

In recent years, studies by neuroscientists have shown that both negative and positive interactions can directly affect the delicate chemical balance and neurological structure of an infant's developing brain. Neuroscientist Lise Eliot cites a study undertaken by researchers at the University of Washington who compared frontal-lobe EEG (electroencephalogram) measures in the infants of depressed and non-depressed mothers. They found that, by about one year of age, babies whose mothers were depressed showed a different pattern of neural responsiveness than control babies. During playful interactions, they experienced less activation of the left hemisphere (the 'feelgood' side) than control babies (Eliot 1999).

Levels of biochemicals such as serotonin (the 'feelgood' hormone) and cortisol (the stress hormone) also vary enormously according to how much positive physical contact children experience:

> Stress in infancy – such as consistently being ignored when you cry – is particularly hazardous because high levels of cortisol in the early months of life can also affect the development of other neurotransmitter systems whose pathways are still being established… When stressed, these various biochemical systems may become skewed in ways that make it more difficult for the individual to regulate himself in later life. (Gerhardt 2004, p.65)

The Massage in Schools programme developed by Mia Elmsäter from Sweden and Sylvie Hétu from Canada is now being used in many UK schools as a way of helping children to build self-esteem and respect for each other. Positive touch, such as this type of massage (which is performed by children on each other and given on the back, head, arms and neck only) releases oxytocin in the brain. This is the hormone known to aid the 'bonding' process after childbirth and it is associated with the regulation of cortisol, having a calming and relaxing effect. Reports from teachers indicate that, among the many benefits of incorporating this programme into the curriculum, children are showing increased concentration levels and decreased levels of agitation and aggression, and are learning skills of empathy and tolerance. Such reports again highlight the advantages of fostering an integrated approach to building healthy self-esteem.

The link between self-esteem and self-concept

In general, psychologists define self-esteem in terms of its relation to our *self-concept*. R.B. Burns offers a neat summary of the complexities of this aspect of ourselves: 'The self concept is a composite image of what we think we are, what we think we can achieve, what we think others think of us and what we would like to be' (Burns 1979, p.vi).

Self-esteem is related to our personal evaluation of our self-concept. It is 'the relative degree of worthiness, or acceptability, which people perceive their self-concept to possess' (Gurney 1988, p.39) and it is inextricably tied up with our early life experiences and the influence of the significant people in our lives. These experiences also affect the images that we form of the *ideal self* – the person we would like to be or think we should be. The difference between the perceived self (self-concept) and the ideal self gives some indication of levels of self-esteem.

In the early years of childhood our self-concept, and therefore our self-esteem, is very malleable and hugely dependant on the way in which we perceive other people's reactions to what we do and say:

> An infant coming into the world has no past, no experience in handling himself, no scale on which to judge his own worth. He must rely on the experiences he has with the people around him and the messages they give him about his worth as a person. (Satir 1972, p.24)

A child with low self-esteem will tend to look for information to confirm his poor view of himself and he may begin to misinterpret what people say and do in order for new experiences to continue to 'fit' his negative self-concept. If he remains dependent on external sources for the maintenance of self-esteem he will find troubles much more difficult to cope with.

> Such a child will develop into an adult who will continue to feel that he has to be successful, or good, or approved of by everyone, if he is to retain any sense of his own value…as though they were entirely dependent for maintaining their self-esteem upon the successes of whatever enterprise was currently

engaging them, without taking into account past blessings or future possibilities. (Storr 1989, p.96)

Undoubtedly, the majority of us will continue to be affected to some degree by these actual or perceived evaluations by others throughout our lives. But in general, if our early experiences have been primarily positive, then eventually we are able to self-evaluate effectively and internalise the feelings of self-worth, and so rely less and less on others for approval and confirmation that we are 'OK'. Our self-awareness and self-reliance in this respect are essential foundation elements for self-esteem (see pp.23–26).

The nature of self-evaluations

To begin with, the self-evaluations of most young children involve descriptions of behaviours, abilities and preferences. They are often unrealistically positive and tend to involve polar opposites of good and bad, including good feelings (emotions) and bad feelings.

In her comprehensive exploration of the 'self', developmental psychologist Susan Harter emphasises the importance of distinguishing between:

> self-evaluations that represent global characteristics of the individual (e.g., 'I am a worthwhile person') and those that reflect the individual's sense of adequacy across particular domains such as one's cognitive competence (e.g., 'I am smart'), social competence (e.g., 'I am well liked by peers'), athletic competence (e.g., 'I am good at sports' and so forth. (Harter 1999, p.5)

The extent to which self-evaluations in various domains affects our global sense of self-worth will depend partly on the level of importance we place on each one.

Not all domains are equally as accessible or as abundant with regard to self-esteem, and levels of self-esteem in different domains may alter according to circumstances. As Coopersmith (1967) and others have noted, natural shifts in self-evaluation can and do occur in different situations and at different times. These changes may be due to the type of task that we are attempting, our mood at the time or the prevailing attitude of the important people in our lives, and for the most part such changes are a normal aspect of healthy self-esteem.

However, some children find these fluctuations more difficult to handle so that negative self-evaluations in specific domains automatically affect global self-esteem, as if the plug has been pulled on the entire self-esteem 'pot'.

Greenier, Kernis and Waschull suggest that:

> People differ not only in whether their level of self-esteem is high or low but also in the extent to which their self-esteem is stable or unstable. These individual differences in stability of self-esteem can be traced to at least two factors... The extent to which people invest their feelings of self-worth in

everyday outcomes and the extent to which their self-concepts are impover-ished. Specifically, it seems likely that the more people invest their feelings of self-worth and the less well developed their self-concepts, the more unstable their self-esteem will be. (Greenier *et al.* 1995, p.67)

Harter points out some significant consequences of using such models (as opposed to concentrating only on global self-perceptions). She notes first that self-report instruments used to draw out domain-specific self-evaluations reveal a distinct gender difference in profiles for males and females, indicating that males are more likely to view themselves favourably in the domains of athletic competence and physical appearance. Also, not all cultures view child-rearing in the same way or have the same concepts of 'self' and self-esteem. As an example, in reviewing the work of Triandis (1972; 1994), Professor Philip Bunard suggests

> students from an individualistic culture, with its emphasis on values such as self-motivation and self-development, may express higher levels of self-esteem than students from collectivist cultures in which emphases are on values such as working together, respect for others and the fulfilment of others' needs. (Bunard 2005, p.85)

Significantly, Harter also notes that children who are physically disabled, or have illnesses such as asthma, diabetes and cancer, often evaluate themselves in a very similar way in various domains to children who are not coping with dis-ability or illness. She proposes several possible reasons for this, including un-conscious denial, confusion between the real and the ideal self, and a reluctance to reveal their true self-perceptions to investigators. It may also be that such children are comparing themselves to other children in a similar situation. Or, most positively, perhaps many children with chronic illness or disability reach a point of healthy adaptation.

> Such children would appear to eschew social comparison in favor of a focus on how they are coping relative to their disorder. As a result, they are able to maintain positive self-evaluations that are both healthy and functional as they meet the challenges imposed by their condition. (Harter 1999, p.139)

It is important to stress that such multi-dimensional models of self-evaluation offer a theoretical perspective. As individuals we do, of course, have a tendency to be more idiosyncratic in the ways that we view ourselves. Thank goodness we don't all fit neatly into theoretical models! However, this does give us a framework from which to explore self-esteem.

Healthy self-esteem is also closely linked with actual and perceived compe-tence and what social learning theorist Albert Bandura called 'self-efficacy': the belief that we are capable of doing something and that we can influence events that affect our lives. Bandura (1977; 1989) suggested that people who have perceptions of high self-efficacy often do better than those who have equal ability but less belief in themselves; they are more likely to persevere with difficult tasks and to use more effective problem-solving strategies; they also have a tendency to set themselves more demanding goals and to focus less on the possible consequences of failure. The level and strength of a person's feelings of self-efficacy can alter according to a variety of factors including specific experiences, verbal persuasion from others and his or her current physiological state.

Bandura also showed how children internalise the standards of those adults who are important to them and how these standards then become self-imposed. He argues that occasionally these self-controlled consequences of behaviour become more powerful than consequences from the external environment: 'there is no more devastating punishment than self-contempt' (Bandura 1971, p.28).

Implications for assessment and intervention

All these factors should be born in mind when structuring appropriate interventions and when considering assessment of self-esteem levels. We need to be aware of which areas of self-esteem we are supporting and how these can have repercussions in other areas, we need to be aware of possible cultural and gender differences and we should be mindful of our own interactions with children and in supporting parents in this process.

With regard to assessments, the current emphasis on outcome measurements and evidence-based practice in so much of our work may lead us to use questionnaires and checklists which have their own limitations. Perhaps the complex nature of self-esteem defies quantifying. Perhaps in the very act of assessing self-esteem we risk being evaluative and risk highlighting areas of concern for children. I am not suggesting that we should not use such instruments as are available, but that we should be vigilant about using them with integrity. (See 'Suggestions for further reading' at the end of this chapter.)

The foundation elements of healthy self-esteem

My observations and clinical experience indicate that there are seven key elements that form the foundation for social and emotional well-being and thereby lead to healthy self-esteem. As a child grows and develops, some of these elements may become more central to his or her feelings of self-worth and competency than others but all of them are needed to some degree. The interaction is reciprocal – healthy levels of self-esteem will enable the consolidation and growth of these seven elements – and the process is ongoing and self-perpetuating. The elements are as follows:

Self-knowledge

This is about finding out who 'I' am and where I fit into the social world around me. It involves:

- understanding differences and commonalities – for example, how I am different from others in looks and character, or how I can have an interest in common with others
- knowing that I can sometimes behave in different ways according to the situation that I'm in and that I have many aspects to my personality
- developing and maintaining my personal values
- developing a sense of my personal history – my own 'story'.

Self and others

This involves:

- understanding the joys and challenges of relationships: learning to co-operate with others, being able to see things from another person's perspective and developing an understanding of how they might see me, and learning respect and tolerance for other people's views
- developing and maintaining my own identity as a separate person while still recognising the natural interdependence of relationships and developing a sense of my familial/cultural 'story'
- understanding my emotions and being aware of the ways in which I express them. For healthy self-esteem I will need to develop a degree of emotional resilience so that I am not overwhelmed by my emotions and so that I can tolerate frustration. I will need to know that I can choose how to express emotions appropriately rather than deny or repress them or act in an inappropriate way. Similarly, I need to be able to recognise other people's emotions and be able to distinguish my feelings from those of others.

Self-acceptance

This involves:

- knowing my own strengths and recognising areas that I find difficult and may want to work on. This includes accepting that it is natural to make mistakes and that this is sometimes how we learn best
- feeling OK about my physical body.

Self-reliance

This involves:

- knowing how to take care of myself, both physically and emotionally, and developing an understanding that life is often difficult but there are many things that I can do to help myself along the path
- building a measure of independence and self-motivation: being able to self-monitor and adjust my actions, feelings and thoughts according to realistic assessments of my progress, and believing that I have mastery over my life and can meet challenges as and when they arise
- reducing my reliance on other people's opinions and evaluations.

Self-expression

This involves:

- understanding how we communicate with each other, including learning to 'read the signals' beyond the words so that I can understand others successfully and also express myself fully and congruently
- developing creativity in self-expression and recognising and celebrating the unique and diverse ways in which we each express who we are.

Self-confidence

This involves:

- knowing that my opinions, thoughts and actions have value and that I have the right to express them
- developing my knowledge and abilities so that I feel able to experiment with different methods of problem-solving and can be flexible enough to alter my strategies if needed
- being able to accept challenges and make choices
- being secure enough in myself to be able to cope successfully with the unexpected.

Self-awareness

Self-awareness is the cornerstone of realistic self-evaluation. It involves:

- developing the ability to be focused in the here and now rather than absorbed in negative thoughts about the past or future
- learning to listen to my body and my emotions so that I am aware of my feelings as they arise
- understanding that emotional, mental and physical changes are a natural part of my life and that I have choices about how I change and develop.

Aspects of each of the seven foundation elements are addressed in Sections II–VIII of the children's activities in Part Three of this book, but these divisions are somewhat arbitrary since in reality all areas are interdependent. There is no activities section for 'self-awareness' for example since this is an integral part of all the other sections. (See also the notes for each element under the relevant session outlines for parents in Part Four).

In summary

There is much that can be done to help children to build and maintain healthy self-esteem in the face of life's many challenges, and to help the child whose fragile sense of self-esteem is already bruised. In more extreme cases, the physiological effects of neglect or lack of loving relationships during babyhood will undoubtedly severely complicate the recovery pattern. The task of helping such troubled children to regain self-esteem or to build self-esteem where none exists is therefore a complex and multi-layered undertaking.

At the same time, we should not underestimate the impact on a child's life of a caring adult who is able to 'be there' for him and to hear his story with acceptance, empathy and wisdom. As facilitators (and this includes parents) we can support children by:

- being curious about their internal monologue (their theory about themselves)
- showing genuine warmth and respect for them as unique individuals
- being fully aware of how our actions and words affect each child's self-concept and therefore his levels of self-esteem
- helping them to develop self-awareness and realisation of how their behaviour affects other people
- helping them to develop the ability to make realistic self-evaluations
- helping them to understand that self-esteem can change in form and intensity according to many different factors, that this is normal and that it need not have a negative effect on their overall sense of self and 'worth-whileness'.

Not a small task by any means, but one that will be infinitely rewarding for those who incorporate this way of being into their daily interactions with children.

References

Ainsworth, M.D.S., Bell, S.M.V. and Stayton, D.J. (1971) 'Individual differences in Strange Situation behaviour of one-year-olds.' In H.R. Schaffer (ed.) *The Origins of Human Social Relations*. New York: Academic Press.

Bandura, A. (1971) *Social Learning Theory*. Englewood Cliffs, NJ: Prentice-Hall.

Bandura, A. (1977) 'Self-efficacy: Toward a unifying theory of behaviour change.' *Psychological Review 84*, 191–215.

Bandura, A. (1989) 'Perceived self-efficacy in the exercise of personal agency.' *The Psychologist: Bulletin of the British Psychological Society 10*, 411–24.

Bowlby, J. (1969) *Attachment and Loss. Volume 1: Attachment.* London: The Hogarth Press and The Institute of Psychoanalysis.

Bunard, P. (2005) *Counselling Skills for Health Professionals* (4th edition). Cheltenham: Nelson Thornes Ltd.

Burns, R.B. (1979) *The Self Concept in Theory, Measurement, Development and Behaviour.* New York: Longman.

Coopersmith, S. (1967) *The Antecedents of Self-Esteem.* San Francisco, CA: W.H. Freeman and Company.

Eliot, L. (1999) *What's Going on in There? How the Brain and Mind Develop in the First Five Years of Life.* New York: Bantam.

Gerhardt, S. (2004) *Why Love Matters. How Affection Shapes a Baby's Brain.* London: Routledge.

Greenier, K.D., Kernis, M.H. and Waschull, S.B. (1995) 'Not all high (or low) self-esteem people are the same. Theory and research on stability of self-esteem.' In M.H. Kerns (ed.) *Efficacy, Agency, and Self-Esteem.* New York and London: Plenum Press.

Gurney, P. (1988) *Self-Esteem in Children with Special Educational Needs.* London and New York: Routledge.

Harter, S. (1999) *The Construction of the Self.* New York: Guilford Press.

Main, M. and Solomon, J. (1990) 'Procedures for identifying infants as disorganised/disorientated during the Ainsworth Strange situation.' In M. Greenberg, D. Cicchetti and M. Cummings (eds) *Attachment During the Preschool Years: Theory, Research and Intervention.* Chicago: University of Chicago Press.

Mruk, C.J. (1999) *Self-Esteem: Research, Theory and Practice* (second edition). London: Free Association Books.

Satir, V. (1972) *Peoplemaking.* London: Souvenir Press.

Storr, A. (1989) *Solitude.* London: Fontana.

Triandis, H.C. (1972) 'Collectivism v. individualism.' In W.B. Gudykunst and Y.Y. Kim (eds) *Readings on Communicating with Strangers.* New York: McGraw Hill.

Triandis, H.C. (1994) 'Cultural syndromes and emotions.' In S. Kitayama and H.R. Markus (eds) *Emotion and Culture: Empirical Studies of Mutual Influence.* Washington, DC: American Psychological Association.

Suggestions for further reading

For a review of self-esteem assessments see:

Butler, R.J. and Gasson, S.L. (2005) 'Self esteem/self concept scales for children and adolescents: A review.' *Child and Adolescent Mental Health 10*, 4, 190–201.

Plummer, D.M. (2007) *Self-Esteem Games for Children.* London: Jessica Kingsley Publishers.

Contacts

For information on the Massage in Schools programme in the UK:

www.massageinschoolsassociation.org.uk

Chapter 3

Working within the School Curriculum

In the 1980s and 1990s, alongside the growth in literature exploring the nature of self-esteem, came a burgeoning interest in the importance of creating a classroom atmosphere that supports this vital aspect of a child's development. This chapter suggests ways of integrating self-esteem activities with other aspects of learning.

If you have been drawn to this book as an educator, then you have probably had many experiences of working with children with low self-esteem. Some of these children appear to place little value on their abilities and often deny their successes. They find it difficult to set goals and to problem-solve. Many give up trying and consequently perform well below their academic and social capabilities: their self-limiting beliefs become a self-fulfilling prophecy.

There are also many children who do achieve at or near their academic potential but have a constant fear of failure and a drive for perfection that may preclude creativity and experimentation. Such a child may set unrealistically high personal goals, thus continually confirming to himself that he is 'no good' each time that he experiences a set-back.

Research in this area has not come up with a definitive answer to the question of which comes first – healthy self-esteem or academic achievement. The two are, undoubtedly, closely interlinked and the relationship may be a reciprocal one:

> Some writers regard self-esteem as a threshold variable…that is to say it may not be as strong or significant in its effect on academic performance when it is at an average or above average level but it seriously inhibits persistence, confidence and academic performance when the child's self-esteem is at a low level. It is therefore argued that, whatever one's assumptions about the direction of causality between low self-esteem and academic achievement, in the case of markedly low self-esteem, one must seek to enhance that first before undertaking any remedial teaching. (Gurney 1988, p.57)

Susan Harter has suggested the value of distinguishing between the *goal* of enhancing self-esteem and the *target* of the interventions. She, and others, argue that skills-based interventions which encourage creative achievement may, as a by-product, produce higher self-esteem that is also more stable:

> [W]hile self-esteem enhancement may be a goal, intervention strategies should be directed at its *determinants*. For example, attempts to impact global self-worth should first identify the specific *causes* of perceived overall worth as a person, in the design of interventions to ameliorate these causes which should, in turn, enhance global feelings of self-worth. (Harter 1999, p.311)

As I mentioned in Chapter 2, there are also those who have argued that the prominence given to self-esteem enhancement is obscuring other aspects of child development and child-rearing, and that it may distract educators from teaching specific skills and deny students the 'buzz' of actual achievements. Once again, I would like to re-emphasise the major tenet of this book in relation to these assertions which is that helping children to build and maintain healthy self-esteem requires an integrated approach; self-esteem is most effectively nurtured through mindful interactions with children *and* through helping them to build specific cognitive, emotional and physical skills relevant to their age and potential abilities.

An important point to remember in relation to this is the heavy reliance that young children place on positive feedback from significant others in their lives – every look, comment and action has potential to contribute to their concept of who they are and their feelings of value and competency. We cannot therefore assume that a child with low self-esteem will suddenly be able to value herself through internalising her academic achievement alone. Her environment, her interactions with others and the way that she interprets these will have a huge part to play.

Teachers are obviously in an excellent position to be able to offer support in this respect.

One of the early proponents of self-esteem oriented learning in the UK was educationalist Peter Gurney. He argued that self-esteem is of central importance as a foundation for learning and should be '*the* prime goal for education' (Gurney 1988, p.78). And in the USA professors of education James Beane and Richard Lipka (1984) wrote:

> Educators are charged with the task of helping young people experience healthy growth and development. Today we know that this means much more than just intellectual and physical growth. If we are to help, we must also define ways of nurturing personal and social growth. At the core of these are the perceptions young people have of themselves. In other words, an educational program without an emphasis on enhancing self-perceptions is an incomplete program. (p.x)

Schools were quick to take up the call and to instigate specific classroom routines and activities to promote the growth and maintenance of self-esteem and, in more recent years, to actively support the development of 'emotional literacy' in their pupils (see suggestions for further reading at the end of this chapter). Many schools also recognised that a truly effective approach to supporting children in this way involves fostering a 'whole-school' atmosphere of respect and self-esteem and that this extends to supporting the self-esteem of school staff and to the involvement of parents as well. Beane and Lipka (1984, p.58) were adamant about this role when they wrote: 'It is clear that if educators are truly concerned with enhancing the self-perception of young people, they must develop improved means for enhancing the expectations parents have for their children and the quality of parent–child interaction.'

Circle-times, which are now an established routine in many classes, do much to address the need for children's learning to be set in the context of a whole-person approach. Many of the activities described in this book can be incorporated into circle-time sessions. Where these are not already in existence, teachers will be able to use the format outlined to create a regular time-slot for this type of interactive sharing and learning if they want to. There is enough material here to span a full academic year if sessions are brief and shorter activities and ideas are incorporated into existing learning strategies. The activity sheets will fulfil many literacy and PSHE learning objectives for Key Stages 1 and 2 in England and Wales and can be adapted for different age groups and ability levels. There is a deliberate mixture of listening, speaking, reading, writing and drawing, as well as individual and group work.

The main aim of the activities is, of course, to help children to develop the seven key foundation elements outlined in Chapter 2. However, within this framework, the activity sheets and expansion activities also aim to:

- foster an atmosphere where children can be actively engaged in the learning process
- encourage spontaneity and creativity
- help focus thought processes
- encourage expansion of vocabulary knowledge
- develop higher-level thinking skills
- provide an opportunity to develop and practise organisational and self-monitoring skills
- encourage tolerance and respect of other people's ideas
- provide a vehicle for positive interaction with peers
- enhance awareness of cause and effect.

The structure provided by having a general theme throughout the sessions, together with repeated patterns of imagery, will help children to establish a familiar format for problem-solving and goal-setting, which they can then be guided to use in a variety of lessons. In this way children can be encouraged in the development of their imaginative and creative skills to support their learning in all areas of academic and social development.

References

Beane, J.A. and Lipka, R.P. (1984) *Self-Concept, Self-Esteem, and the Curriculum.* Columbia University, NY: Teachers College Press.

Gurney, P. (1988) *Self-Esteem in Children with Special Educational Needs.* London and New York: Routledge.

Harter, S. (1999) *The Construction of the Self.* New York: Guilford Press.

Suggestions for further reading

Antidote (2003) *The Emotional Literacy Handbook. Promoting Whole-School Strategies.* London: David Fulton Publishers.

Robinson, G. and Maines, B. (1989) 'A self-concept approach to dealing with pupils.' In R. Evans (ed.) *Special Educational Needs 'Policy and Practice'.* Oxford: Blackwell Education in association with National Association for Remedial Education.

Chapter 4

The Child with Speech and Language Difficulties

With some occasional adaptations, the activity sheets and expansion ideas are suitable for use by children with a range of disabilities. This chapter focuses on self-esteem in relation to communication delay and disorders. It is intended as a brief introduction to this area for professionals other than speech and language therapists who may be involved in working with children who have a communication impairment.

Estimates suggest that between 14 per cent and 20 per cent of pre-school children have delayed or deviant speech or language while studies of problems in speech, language, voice and fluency (e.g. stuttering) in school-aged children suggest an average prevalence rate of 5 per cent (Royal College of Speech and Language Therapists 2006).

Self-esteem can so easily be affected when children have to cope with specific difficulties such as speech and language delay or disorder.

Our speech is naturally full of ambiguities and often our verbal messages don't match our non-verbal communication. We expect children to learn the subtleties of our ways of communicating through listening and observation, rather than through specific teaching; but the child with speech and language difficulties may find this extremely difficult and can often misinterpret messages. Mistakes in interpreting and using non-verbal communication can lead to a child feeling isolated and confused.

The child with a speech or language difficulty will have had countless experiences of not understanding what is being said to him or of others not understanding what he is saying. He may have experienced people looking at him blankly, asking 'What did he say?' over his head or, worst of all, laughing at his speech efforts or teasing him. The child who stutters, for example, is often acutely aware of the effect that his struggle to speak may be having on some of his listeners – effects ranging from impatience to mirth, sympathy and sometimes physical tension. Each of these experiences has potential to erode his self-esteem.

Furthermore, although children with communication difficulties may well have average or above-average intelligence, others (adults as well as peers) often view them as 'not very bright'. Once this concept has been formed and transmitted to a child he may become resigned to it or give up trying to compete and begin instead to underachieve because this fits in with how he is expected to behave. Even relatively mild communication impairments can thereby have far-reaching effects on self-esteem, interpersonal relationships and classroom performance.

Not only do children take note of other people's comments, they also need to develop the ability to use language in a way that helps them to define their successes and difficulties. For those who have limited speech or language skills, 'the inability to negotiate with others verbally, to stake one's claim to attributes that others are ignoring, or to deny an attribution that seems unfair, for example, means that the elaboration of self-concepts is impeded' (Dalton 1994, p.3).

When planning any type of self-esteem support strategies we therefore also need to take account of the fact that language primarily performs a social function. Many of the activities offered here are aimed at promoting this social use of language. In particular, conversation skills (starting, maintaining and ending a conversation), identification and expression of emotions, and descriptions of objects. Studies indicate that these areas can significantly improve with therapy (e.g. Richardson and Klecan-Aker 2000).

Although I have run groups specifically for children with speech and language difficulties, including these children in whole-class activities based on building and maintaining self-esteem has potential to have an equal, if not more profound, effect. They will be able to see that they are not the only ones who have doubts and uncertainties about their abilities; they are not the only ones who have to develop strategies to cope with teasing and so on. Such joint activities will also help others in the group to develop an understanding of how children might feel in relation to their speech or language difficulty and to appreciate the diversity of ways in which we communicate with each other.

By specifically giving children the chance to learn to read signals more accurately and to understand more about themselves and their abilities, we can support and encourage their learning and their self-esteem. The repetitive nature of the exercises presented here is intended to particularly help in this process. All the activity sheets can be adapted to suit varying levels of language and general ability.

References

Dalton, P. (1994) *Counselling People with Communication Problems*. London: Sage.

Richardson, K. and Klecan-Aker, J.S. (2000) 'Teaching pragmatics to language-learning disabled children: A treatment outcome study.' *Child Language Teaching and Therapy 16*, 23–42.

Royal College of Speech and Language Therapists (2006) *Communicating Quality 3*, London: Royal College of Speech and Language Therapists.

Suggestion for further reading

Fleming, P., Miller, C. and Wright, J. (1997) *Speech and Language Difficulties in Education: Approaches to Collaborative Practice for Teachers and Speech and Language Therapists*. Bicester: Winslow Press.

Chapter 5

Guidelines for Facilitators

Whether you are working with an individual child, setting up a group for the first time or working with an established group or class, there are some general guidelines that will be helpful to keep in mind. This chapter delineates key points related to structuring the activities for maximum effect.

Working with a child individually

Since self-esteem is so intimately connected with our experiences with others, the main emphasis of the instructions in Part Two of this book is on group work. However, there will undoubtedly be occasions when a child with low self-esteem is being supported on a one-to-one basis. In this instance the discussions can still be carried out between the facilitator and child and there are plenty of expansion activities that need not necessarily involve groups of children working together.

Working with a group

Because new groups need time to get to know each other it is useful to build up a repertoire of group 'gelling' games and warm-up games. Devoting some specific time to these games will help children to feel more relaxed about sharing their ideas and taking part in co-operative activities. See, for example, *Social Skills and the Speech Impaired* (Rustin and Kuhr 1989) or *Self-Esteem Games for Children* (Plummer 2007).

It is also useful to establish a set of group 'rules', and to remind the group of these periodically if needed. Such rules might include the following:

- Only one person talks at a time.
- Don't talk to other children during the imagery exercises.
- Respect other people's pictures and ideas.
- There is no such thing as a wrong image.

Whatever children produce as a result of these activities, there should not, of course, be any judgement made in terms of achievement. Although some children may need guidance to help them to participate in a co-operative and creative dialogue with their peers and with the adult who is structuring the session, nothing that is said or produced during this time can ever be 'wrong'. It is important that children understand this rule right from the start so that they feel comfortable about making contributions.

Children are very used to hearing themselves talked about, especially in therapy or classroom exchanges between professionals and parents. Sometimes, however, it is appropriate for children to be able to say things openly and to know that the information will not be passed on (except, of course, in relation to child protection issues). Respecting a child's contributions can so easily include asking permission to share their work and ideas with others, rather than assuming that it is OK to do so.

Family therapist Virginia Satir wrote:

> Feelings of worth can only flourish in an atmosphere where individual differences are appreciated, mistakes are tolerated, communication is open, and rules are flexible – the kind of atmosphere that is found in a nurturing family. (Satir 1972, p.26)

I can think of no better maxim to take on board in the running of a self-esteem group!

Organising the activities
Activity sheets

You will find separate notes in Part Two for each of the activity sheets. These outline the aims and offer ideas on how to present the activities. I have occasionally quoted the experiences of some of the children I have seen for therapy. Their names and personal details have been altered but their comments and images are genuine.

The activities are divided into eight sections around the theme of collecting precious treasure for a magician's treasure chest. As mentioned in the Introduction, this theme is easily altered for older children who may respond well to the idea of collecting skills or to the familiar concept of collecting tools for a toolbox. The activities follow a logical sequence in order to provide a basic grounding in the foundation elements of self-esteem but can also be used separately according to individual needs and preferences. However, even if you are only intending to use a limited selection of activities it is recommended that you include the relevant introductory sheet for each section that you choose.

Most of the activity sheets can be adapted for discussion or drawing for those who struggle with writing, and there are plenty of very practical activities. You might also offer to be a secretary and let children dictate what they want to say if resources permit.

In preference, I would encourage children to draw as many of the images as possible, especially those children who do not think that they are able to draw well.

It is important to give children the opportunity to experiment with drawing images of different sizes and to use different media. For this reason, I suggest that images are produced on separate pieces of paper wherever this is feasible and that children should be allowed to choose the size and colour of paper that they want to use.

Brainstorms

The idea of the brainstorms is to accept all ideas to begin with, allowing each child to contribute as much as possible without fear of judgement or 'getting it wrong'. When enough ideas have been gathered, the next stage is to encourage objective analysis (e.g. 'So, if you did this, what would happen then? How do you think you would feel?') and then to come to a consensus about the most useful ideas.

Expansion activities

These expansion activities are an integral part of the process of using imagery. They are important because they help children to connect the inner world of images to the outer world of the here and now, and in this way to gradually integrate what they have learnt into their lives. I recommend using as many of the expansion activities as possible and involving the children in inventing some for themselves.

Imagery exercises

Many of the activity sheets involve the children in creating their own images to represent various ideas and feelings. There are specific instructions in Part Two for facilitating these imagery exercises. If you would like to explore this further then more detailed guidelines for longer imagery exercises can be found in *Using Interactive Imagework with Children* (Plummer 1999, pp.59–67).

Using stories

One of the main attractions of using stories to help children to develop self-awareness and appropriate coping strategies is that they are one step removed from reality, such that it is possible to explore issues and emotions in a feeling of safety. If a child has taken a liking to a particular story, it may be for a reason that she has not yet realised. Bettelheim suggests that some fairy tales, for example, get across to the child the idea that 'struggle against severe difficulties in life is unavoidable, is an intrinsic part of human existence – but that if one does not shy away, but steadfastly meets unexpected and often unjust hardships, one masters all obstacles and at the end emerges victorious' (Bettelheim 1978, p.8).

In each section of Part Two, I have suggested a variety of children's storybooks to supplement the activity sheets. These are primarily for the younger age range (seven to eight years) but there are also some suggestions for 9–11-year-olds. For this older age group, books such as those by Jacqueline Wilson (e.g. *The Story of Tracy Beaker*) and Judy Blume (e.g. *Superfudge*) also contain a wealth of insights into coping with change and coping with difficulties. (All the books listed were available at the time of writing this edition.)

Of course, a story produced by children themselves can also be incredibly powerful. Such stories may be only a few words or sentences in length and yet convey how a child is thinking and feeling with great clarity and precision. Once again, such stories do not need to be interpreted by adults in order for a child to be able to benefit from the process – they can simply be a vehicle for expression and personal understanding. Sometimes I do specifically co-author a story with children in order to help them to explore dilemmas and to solve particular problems, but the characters, events and feelings are always originally provided by them rather than suggested by me.

Materials

These are the basic materials you will need for the expansion activities (each section also has a list of any additional materials required for specific activities):

- a flip chart or whiteboard and pens
- plenty of plain white and coloured paper for drawing images
- large poster-sized paper for joint collages
- glue
- scissors
- coloured pencils/felt tips
- a children's dictionary.

A final thought

Helping children to build self-esteem is not the same as encouraging a reluctant acceptance of 'this is who I am'. Nor is it the same as encouraging bragging or aggression ('I'm OK and you're not'). The opposite of low self-esteem might quite simply be 'a quiet pleasure in being one's self' (Rogers 1961, p.87). This is the gift that we can offer to children in our care: whether it is a timely smile, a few words of support or a full self-esteem course, we really can make a difference.

References

Bettelheim, B. (1978) *The Uses of Enchantment*. Harmondsworth: Penguin.

Plummer, D. (1999) *Using Interactive Imagework with Children. Walking on the Magic Mountain*. London: Jessica Kingsley Publishers.

Plummer, D. (2007) *Self-Esteem Games for Children*. London: Jessica Kingsley Publishers.

Rogers, C. (1961) *On Becoming a Person: A Therapist's View of Psychotherapy*. London: Constable.

Rustin, L. and Kuhr, A. (1989) *Social Skills and the Speech Impaired*. London: Taylor and Francis.

Satir, V. (1972) *Peoplemaking*. London: Souvenir Press.

Suggestions for further reading

Dwivedi, K.N. (ed.) (1997) *The Therapeutic Use of Stories*. London and New York: Routledge.

Paley, V.G. (1991) *The Boy who would be a Helicopter*. London: Harvard University Press.

Part Two

Instructions for Self-Esteem Activities

I

Getting Started
(STARS and EMERALDS)

STARS
Aims of this section

- to introduce the concept of images
- to establish reward systems
- to acknowledge each child's current achievements
- to identify individual goals
- to set up an appropriate format for discussion, according to age and ability levels of the group

Additional materials

- coloured paper for making stars
- small box or bowl
- suitable materials, such as A4 card and treasury tags, for making individual folders
- hole punch
- glitter and stickers or alternatives for decorating folders

Activity worksheets
1. What are images? (p.101)

This introductory sheet can be used as a basis for a group discussion. Allow each child the chance to contribute an idea that he feels came from his imagination.

Compare and contrast the images that the children have. Talk about all the different *types* of possible images. For example, some will be like pictures, some will be sounds (like imagining a conversation or a tune in your head), some will be feeling or sensation images (like imagining the feel of velvet or mud). See Part One, Chapter 1.

2. Finding some magic (p.102)

Read this sheet together and talk about what it means. Encourage children to put forward their own ideas and to suggest other things that could be 'magic treasure'. Sunil (aged 11), for example, came up with 'respecting others' as being an important treasure to have.

3. My personal record of achievements (p.103)

For a long time I used stars and stickers for rewards in the groups that I ran, believing that children needed some physical confirmation that they were managing to achieve their targets. However, the drawback to this was that it invariably became a competition with much counting and recounting of who had managed to get the most of the treasured stickers. Children would actually come and ask me for another sticker 'because I've just kept good eye contact when I asked you'! The more wily amongst them would assure other therapists in the group that I had told them to go claim a sticker from them!

In the end I decided on a different system. I use the stars printed on pp.103–104. Children are told that when *everyone* has achieved a certain number of stars there will be an award ceremony. To avoid individuals being singled out by their peers as trailing behind, I make sure that everyone more or less keeps pace with their stars (although they may be rewarded for very diverse reasons). I also encourage children to point out to me when they think other members of the group have done particularly well in working towards their targets.

The praise that you write in the stars needs to be as specific as possible. 'Well done' has much less of an impact than 'I can see that you have put a lot of thought into your picture. You have used some really interesting shapes and colours' or 'Your "problem" picture really shows me what it must feel like to stutter. This is what I call artistic.' This may be too wordy for some, but I have watched children reading their stars with broad smiles and mutter such things as 'cool' whereas their response to briefer, non-descriptive praise has been neutral or fleeting at best. (See also the discussion of confidence groups on pp.44–47).

Talk about the meaning of the word 'achievement' and then let children look it up in a dictionary if needed. Make sure that everyone has thought of one recent achievement to write in his or her first star. Share these in the group. This can be done in several ways. For example:

- Celebrate the achievement in some way, e.g. a round of applause as each one is read out.

- Split the group into pairs so that they can read out each other's achievements.

- Photocopy the stars or get the children to make separate ones. Rewrite their achievements and put them on a wall poster with each child's name underneath.

(See also expansion activities for this section.)

In the same way that you are specific with your praise, it is important to encourage children to be specific about their own achievements. For example: 'I scored two goals last week in the school football match' or 'I made up an imaginative story about _____'.

Although some children might find it difficult to recognise their current abilities, achievements and talents, this is always a good starting point before moving on to thinking about learning targets and future goals. In fact it is important to continue to acknowledge and celebrate current strengths throughout all the sections.

It seems that children often have very little time in their lives to celebrate where they are at before moving on to the next challenge, the next learning target, the next physical achievement – almost as though we are telling them, 'Yes, well done, but that's still not quite good enough'! Sometimes verbalising our admiration can enable a child to self-evaluate in a wonderfully productive way: 'How did you know how to do that?', 'I had no idea that you knew about the planets/were so artistic/could make a kite. Was that hard to learn?', 'Tim said that you always remember people's birthdays – that's really impressive! How do you manage to do that?'

There is one more aspect of praise which is significant in terms of group processes (this includes families). The *absence* of praise may have almost as much of a detrimental effect on some vulnerable children as the giving of negative comments. When a vulnerable child hears others in the group being praised by an important adult for attributes and talents which he admires but does not feel he possesses (and is not being praised for) this gives indirect information to that child about how the adult views him. So whilst we need to keep praise realistic and honest, we also need to find out what really matters to individual children. What do they most admire in others? What would they most like to be praised for? How could we support them in nurturing their wishes in this respect? See notes for expansion activity (e) in this section and GOLD activity sheets, particularly Sheets 1 and 9 and the accompanying notes.

4. Things I would like to achieve (p.105)

This could be achievements related to the specific focus of the group, general achievements or a mixture of both.

Do this as a brainstorm either with the whole group or in smaller groups, depending on numbers. Allow time for children to write out their own ideas from the joint list. A fairly typical list from a speech and language therapy group for children who stutter is:

- To be more confident with my speaking.
- To speak in a voice that people can hear.
- To stop stuttering (not always achievable but acknowledged as a very genuine wish).
- To talk more calmly.
- To be able to answer the register.
- To be more relaxed.
- To get to know some more people who are like me.
- To be able to talk in front of a group.
- To make some new friends.
- To have fun.
- To learn more about speaking.

Individual children will probably end up with a mixture of realistic aims and some that are not achievable within the time that you spend together. This can be discussed so that they can choose which aims to focus on. Try to avoid being overly realistic at this point – even amazing dreams for the future can at least be acknowledged as an exciting thought!

Expansion activities

(a) Establish a regular format to encourage realistic self-awareness and peer feedback

One of the most effective ways in which this can be carried out is within the framework of confidence groups. The idea for these groups is based on the format for oekos or 'home' groups, which are an established element of imagework training, combined with aspects of techniques developed by Lee Glickstein (1998) as a means of personal development in public speaking. An outline of an oekos group format for adults and adolescents can be found in Plummer 2005, pp.49–50. Glickstein's work is well-known in the UK as a self-help tool for adults who stutter. Specialist speech and language therapists Carolyn Desforges and Louise Tonkinson (2006) have also developed a particular version of his approach which they use with children. With their kind permission I have taken some of the principles that they outline and have altered the format to fit with the ethos of imagework and self-esteem enhancement to create confidence groups. These might be used after a discussion, imagework activity, role play, story or other expansion activity which has highlighted particular skills for the children to try out. See also notes for GOLD Activity Sheets 6, 7 and 8.

Format for confidence groups

Where you are working with large numbers of children (e.g. a class) this works best if you split into smaller groups. I have facilitated confidence groups with up to 12 children participating, but obviously the size of the group depends partly on the length of time available and partly on the number of facilitators/helpers who know the format.

Stage one

For these groups to work there are three principles which need to be established with the children from the outset:

1. *Focus on the positive.* When each child takes part in the group, whether giving or receiving feedback, he or she is reminded and encouraged to focus on skills not deficits.

2. *The group members offer support to the speaker.* This is discussed with the children in terms of what 'support' means and how we show support and acceptance of others, particularly how we show acceptance non-verbally by fully listening.

3. *The speaker 'connects' with the audience.* This is established by helping children to focus on eye contact and breathing calmly. Children are encouraged to both sense the acceptance from their audience and to be aware of physical ways in which this is shown. This may seem a difficult concept for some at first but they can be reassured that there is no right or wrong way of doing this.

The children sit in a circle and are invited to relax and to 'tune into' themselves ('Notice what your body is feeling… Notice where your thoughts are drifting to… Be aware of the other people in the small group then tune back into yourself again').

The first round in the group generally doesn't involve any speaking at all. Instead, the children each take a turn to walk up to the 'stage' (an identified space in the circle). They make slow eye contact with each of the group members in the audience and then walk back to their seat. The audience return eye contact and silently 'send' their complete acceptance. The 'speaker' is asked to be open to receive this acceptance. When the child has returned to his or her seat, specific, truthful feedback is given by the group facilitators on looking confident, walking in a confident way, using calm breathing to settle them-selves, gaining support by using eye contact etc. The same format can be used with the children remaining seated and taking turns around the circle if this is more appropriate.

Stage two

The children take turns to walk up to the speaker position. They give and receive natural, gentle eye contact to everyone in turn and can then choose whether or not to say one small sentence. They could perhaps introduce themselves or say something that they like, or just say 'hello' before returning to their chairs. This time feedback is given primarily from group members with a small amount of feedback from facilitators. The facilitators then praise the group members for the content and quality of the positive feedback given.

Stage three

The children walk up to the speaker position, take time to settle themselves, look around at the audience and then say one or two sentences appropriate to the theme for the day. Once again, the other members of the group simply listen. The speaker is then given feedback by facilitators and group members on particular skills as appropriate. In this section, for example, the skill might be 'acknowledging one of my successes to the whole group' and the speaker might say something like 'I swam two lengths of the swimming pool yesterday'. The children are not focusing on the achievement being acknowledged but instead are encouraged to give very specific feedback about *what the speaker has just done*, such as 'You smiled when you told us that and you looked as though you felt really good about your success', 'You were very brave to go first and speak in front of the whole group', or 'You were great when you let X have a go before you'. Facilitators might include comments such as 'When you told us about your success I felt really proud of you'.

Of course this sort of descriptive feedback will come from adult facilitators to start with in order to give an appropriate model, but as you work through the sections children will quickly recognise all the different things they can praise in relation to each foundation element. Facilitators continue to praise group members for their positive feedback ('You picked up on a very important point in your feedback'; 'You are really noticing how people show their feelings' etc.).

Stage four

Throughout the course you can gradually increase the time for each person to speak when this feels right but maximum time should be around two minutes. Keep an eye on the time to ensure that everyone gets an equal go.

Confidence groups aim to emphasise and promote existing skills as well as developing new skills. They promote connectedness with peers in a very meaningful way – giving children a forum in which to be heard and accepted by their peers and giving them the opportunity to learn how to receive acceptance and 'positive regard' from others.

My own experience of using this format is that it has proved to be an invaluable tool – the children love doing it and the respect and empathy generated between children has a marked effect in other situations. Their ability to self-monitor and self-evaluate in a realistic way is enhanced and the positive feedback from peers is a major boost to self-esteem. Of course, once demonstrated and practised, the principles of focusing on specific skills, connecting with others in order to really 'receive' praise and respect, and the giving of positive, specific feedback can all be used in situations other than a planned confidence group. (See Part Four, 'Working with Parents', particularly Activity Sheet 2.1 and the accompanying notes.)

(b) Each child makes a paper star and writes on it one thing that he or she enjoys doing (anonymously)

Put all the stars in a box or bowl. Take out one at a time and read it. Each child (or at least five or six at a time if you are running a large group) completes the sentence as though she had written it herself, giving a reason for enjoying the activity. Children may need encouragement to think of reasons other than 'because I'm good at it'!

> Patrick (aged nine) completed the sentence 'I enjoy playing the keyboard' with 'because I have wobbly hands' (he explained that this meant he could move his fingers very fast!).

This exercise encourages children to recognise and be accepting of the range of activities that other people enjoy, and to think about *why* they might enjoy them. It also gives them the chance to find out a little about any interests they might have in common and to think about some new activities to try for themselves. Ask the owner of each star to reveal her identity and then ask for a show of hands as to who else likes the same thing. All the stars should eventually be read aloud and returned to their owners. They could then be mounted on one large 'sky' picture and displayed on the wall.

Note: Spend time making and decorating the folders ready for all the activity sheets. I have found that children usually take more care of their folders if they make their own than if they are provided with one.

EMERALDS
Aims of this section

- to explore imagery and the basic imagework format
- to introduce or expand on the concept of awareness of others
- to introduce the idea that what we think affects how we feel

Additional materials

No additional materials are required for this section.

Activity worksheets

1. Imagining (p.106)

Read the exercise 'Think of a chocolate cake' slowly, with plenty of pauses for the children to really explore the images. Whenever possible, ask for verbal feedback while you are doing imagery exercises. This will encourage children actually to *do* the exercise rather than just sit with their eyes closed! For example, when you say 'What does it (the cake) look like?', the group can be asked to describe the sort of chocolate cake they are imagining. Validate the responses by repeating back what you have heard the child say or by making some appropriate sound (Mmmmmm!). The interaction might go something like:

'You see the cake on a big plate... Would anyone like to say what their chocolate cake looks like?'

'It's got Smarties on.'

'Simon's cake has Smarties.'

'Squidgy.'

'Mmmm – a squidgy cake for Craig.'

When you have finished the exercise, discuss similarities and differences in the responses. Reassure children that there is no right or wrong answer. If anyone seems unable to 'see' images that's OK. In my experience, however, children are usually very quick to produce visual images.

Talk about how sometimes we can experience a feeling just by imagining something. (See also Part One, Chapter 1.)

2. Talking cats (p.107)

If we do something regularly, we stop thinking about it too much after a while and just do it automatically but we can still imagine it or recall the pictures from our mind when we want to. When something new is about to happen we can imagine what it might be like. We can also imagine things that we know will never happen at all. This leads on to the next exercise.

3a. Becoming a cat (p.108)

3b. Being a cat (p.109)

This activity helps children to understand a little bit more about how we can construct things in our imagination and, for the older children, could lead on to discussion about seeing events and people's actions and words from different perspectives (i.e. what we construct might not always be accurate). See notes for RUBIES Activity Sheet 12.

I have suggested that the children dictate what they want to say about being a cat, but this is obviously only possible if you have a group of able writers or enough helpers to act as 'secretaries'. Alternatively, discuss Sheet 3a in the group and expand on the vocabulary. Give Sheet 3b to do individually or as a 'do at home' activity.

Expansion activities

(a) Read a story about the imagination

And to Think That I Saw It on Mulberry Street by Dr Seuss is a little boy's tale of his journey from school to home. He wants to tell his dad what he has seen but he thinks that the horse and wagon that he spotted is far too boring to report. By the time he gets home this simple sight has grown into the most amazing tale imaginable!

The Afterdark Princess by Annie Dalton (shortlisted for the Carnegie Medal) is another good read for older children. Joe Quail is an anxious boy who is easily worried by things. When Alice comes to babysit she gives him moonglasses and shows him the Kingdom of the Afterdark. Joe finds the hero in himself when he is called upon to save the last princess of the Afterdark. Also in this series are *The Dream Snatcher* and *The Midnight Museum*.

(b) Talk about what it would be like to be different animals

(c) Set the children the task of finding out about emeralds. What colour are they? Where are they found? What are they used for?

(d) Choose some famous people and talk about what it would be like to be them. What sort of day would they have? Where would they live? What would they eat for breakfast? What would they wear?

(e) Invite the children to choose someone important in their life (parent, brother, sister, friend, grandparent, teacher etc.) and write about what they think would be a typical day for them or draw some things that they would do, wear, eat, etc.

These last two activities encourage not only use of the imagination but also awareness, acceptance and empathy with others. Activity (e) also links with the concept of a 'special adult' or 'sensitive witness'. This is someone other than a parent who is significant in a child's life. Various studies have highlighted the fact that many children have a special adult in their life who offers them emotional and practical support and confirmation of self-worth. These special adults are typically unconditional in their acceptance of the child: in other words, their acceptance is not conditional upon the child fulfilling the adult's expectations.

References

DesForges, C., Tonkinson, L. and Kelly, S. (2006) 'Using the power of speaking circles to develop confident communication.' *Speaking Out*, Spring, 6–7.

Glickstein, L. (1998) *Be Heard Now!* Tap into Your Inner Speaker and Communicate with Ease. New York: Broadway Books.

Plummer, D. (1995) *Helping Adolescents and Adults to Build Self-Esteem*. London: Jessica Kingsley Publishers.

II

Who Am I? (RUBIES)

Aims of this section

- to explore the concept of 'me' and 'not me'
- to understand how people are different and alike
- to introduce the idea that change is possible
- to encourage children to celebrate who they are

Additional materials

- enough hand mirrors for children to share
- silver paper or suitable alternative for making a 'magic mirror' (see expansion activities)
- a cloth or cloak to use for storytelling (see expansion activities)

Activity worksheets

Introductory page (p.111)

Note: It is useful for every child to have all the relevant introductory pages, even if you don't plan to use all the activity sheets in each section.

Talk about how the picture in the mirror might be different each time it is drawn. For example, the child may have a different expression, or be wearing different clothes or a crown made up of the jewels being collected, or perhaps he will be holding something or doing something that shows what he has been learning.

1. The magic mirror (p.112)

Use photos, or look in hand mirrors, and draw self-portraits. This exercise encourages physical self-awareness. The magic mirror can be used for more than physical aspects, however. It appears at the end of each of the following sections where it can be used to help children to identify some of the changes they are making. See note to the introductory page (above).

2. If I were an animal (p.113)

This exercise uses one of the basic formats of imagework (e.g. Glouberman 2003) – *becoming* the image in order to find out more about it. This might also help you to gain more insight into how the children perceive themselves or how they would *like* to be.

Read the passage out to the group slowly to give them time to think about it. If you are running a relatively small group, ask for verbal feedback: 'Would anyone like to tell me what animal they are?' or 'Who wants to tell us what they wish for as this animal?' (See notes for EMERALDS Activity Sheet 1, p.48.) This encourages a feeling of connection between group members and will help you to know what's going on. It also gives more time to those who need to explore images more deeply or are having problems getting an image in the first place. Invariably, the group will not all be working at the same pace. Move on when it feels right to do so.

In large groups, when you are waiting for children to produce their own images, ask them to raise a finger when they have got an image, rather than asking them to call out. There is certainly no 'right' or 'wrong' way for a child to do imagework. Positive encouragement may help her to verbalise what she is experiencing but it is important not to insist that she shares something with you if she doesn't want to. I recommend that you allow your own images to emerge while you are reading, as this will help you to pace the instructions.

When you have completed the exercise make a joint list of the descriptive words that the children used.

Talk about the admired animal's characteristics. Relate some of these to everyday experiences where appropriate. An admired characteristic might be 'fast' and you could talk about times when children are physically fast or when they are quick-thinking, etc. (But see Chapter 1, p.14, with reference to interpreting individual images. This is an exploratory discussion, not an image analysis!)

3. Describing people (p.114)

Brainstorm descriptive words and phrases. Write them all on a flip chart or whiteboard. The only rule is that there should be no 'evaluative' words (i.e. these are objective descriptions not judgements). Talk about how people are unlikely to change most physical features from one day to the next but could, for example, change the length of their hair, have their ears pierced or have a tattoo. Other aspects (e.g. how they act, feel, dress) can change from moment to moment. Someone who is described as thoughtful might sometimes do something that is NOT thoughtful! Most people, however, have a 'usual' way of being. The way in which our moods can change and we can 'act out of character' is an important concept which will be revisited in later sessions. It is crucial for children to realise that it is normal to feel unhappy, grumpy, etc. sometimes and that these feelings will pass.

You may also feel that this is an appropriate point at which to talk with older children about body image and the image of the 'ideal' body shape often portrayed in the media.

See also SILVER Activity Sheets 4 and 5 and the accompanying notes on feelings (pp.62–63).

4. My group (p.115)

This activity sheet needs to be followed up by discussion in the group. This will help to promote not only group identity but also individual self-esteem. Talk about how it is possible to think that someone feels a certain way but that may not be how they see themselves. For example, a child might appear to be very clever but he might think that he is *not* clever compared to an older brother or sister.

Unrealistic comparisons could also be discussed with children in association with Activity 12 in this section and GOLD Activity Sheet 3.

You might suggest that each child collects three descriptions that he likes from what others have written about him and writes these next to his first magic mirror picture. These descriptive words or phrases could also be used to start off Activity Sheet 5.

5. This is me (p.116)

See notes for Activity Sheets 3 and 4 in this section.

Encourage decorations on this activity sheet!

Invite the children to read out their own descriptions in large or small groups. Start with: 'My name is _____. This is how I would like to be described.'

Alternatively, read out a selection (with permission from the children) and see if the rest of the group can guess who is being described.

6. I am me (p.117)

Self-characterisation promotes greater awareness of self and others. It is based on an idea developed by personal construct psychologists and therapists. (See Fransella and Dalton 1990, pp.53–56, for further information.)

Looking through the completed sheets will help you to pick out important themes in how the children see themselves, what worries them, what they enjoy doing, etc. Some children may find this exercise quite difficult, having little idea of how others might see them, or indeed how they see themselves. They may need some prompts in the form of questions such as: 'What would your best friend say about the way that you _____?', 'What helps you to feel good about yourself?'

7. Everyone is different (p.118)

Invite fantastical answers to this as well as more logical ones! Think about 'sameness' in such things as looks, actions, likes and dislikes. Discuss similarities and differences in the answers that are given. Expand on some of the themes by asking questions such as: 'Why would that be difficult?… And *then* what would happen?'

> A group of boys who stutter (9–12 years old) were asked to do this as a homework activity. Almost all of them wrote that if everyone was the same then we would all be fluent and no one would be teased about their speech. One of the group, however, wrote that if we were all the same then everyone would stutter, and what would not be so good about this would be that he would no longer be 'different' or 'special'. Only one child came up with ideas unrelated to speech.

8. Something in common? (p.119)

Although each of us is a unique individual we do, of course, have things in common with others as well. Feeling that we are part of a group, and being accepted and appreciated by a group, gives us a sense of belonging and helps us to feel good about ourselves, especially when our internal reserves are low. Sometimes, however, we may find ourselves behaving in ways that don't truly reflect our self-concept in order to *appear* to fit in with a group. Children can be particularly vulnerable to this sort of peer pressure. They may try to 'fit in' with a group because they think they ought to or because it's 'cool' or it's exciting. There may be times when this is OK and also times when it's not OK, when trying to fit in leads to them feeling awkward or unhappy. In the long term, of course, this can lead to a lowering of self-esteem rather than an increase.

It is important to acknowledge this natural wish to feel accepted and liked and to explore successful ways of achieving this. This activity is a first step towards this exploration. The theme of friendships and groups is developed more fully in Section III (SILVER).

Talk about different areas of 'commonality'. For example, any other groups that the children might be members of – school groups, family groups, sports teams, etc. The aim is to help the children to look beyond physical things that they might have in common to such things as leisure interests and shared aims.

9. Making a change (p.120)

Imagining that you have already achieved a goal can be more powerful than planning what you will have to do beforehand. Athletes are often trained to see themselves having made the perfect high jump, having achieved their personal best time, and so on. This activity sheet introduces a concept that will be used in more depth in later sections.

Talk about how things don't always turn out as we expect. I may have wished to change how I look, but then I found that when the change happened no one recognised me and I had to make friends with people all over again! Or I wished I could be faster at running so I didn't keep missing the school bus, and then I won an inter-school race!

10. The change shop (p.121)

It is important to recognise parts of us that we're not happy about. This is a way of children being more accepting of who they are now so that they will be more able and ready to make changes.

Before you start this activity sheet give a few examples, such as 'I would like to sell my curly hair and exam nerves and buy a bagful of confidence for when I sing in the school play'.

Encourage elaborate descriptions of the shop and the shopkeeper. Talk about what sort of person the shopkeeper might be (e.g. very careful, friendly, sensitive) as he is going to help children to get rid of unwanted things and buy or change them for things that they really want.

Share some ideas when the activity sheets are completed. Talk about how things that some people want to sell, others might have wanted to buy. See if there is anything that can be exchanged between children. For more able children you could expand on this by holding a group 'auction' of carefully selected characteristics (i.e. only auction characteristics that someone else is likely to bid for).

11. Things I like about me (p.122)

This activity sheet provides an opportunity to recap and bring together all the points already identified and discussed. Encourage children to include physical attributes (e.g. 'I like my hair') as well as personality attributes (e.g. 'I'm a good friend').

I have sometimes used this exercise too near the beginning of a course and have found that the children struggle to identify more than one or two things that they like about themselves. Some are unable to name even one. By leaving it until later, when they have had plenty of time to discuss the previous activity sheets, you can avoid the potential pitfall of children becoming disheartened in their struggle to complete a list of this sort.

See also GOLD Activity Sheets 1 and 2.

12. Important people (p.123)

This activity can be extended to discussing and drawing important events, places and objects. Identifying important aspects of their life helps children to develop awareness of the effect that their environment and experiences have on how they see themselves.

This could also lead on to discussions about how different people see the same things in different ways. For example, three people seeing a fight in the playground will all have slightly different versions of events according to their own preconceptions and perhaps their alliances with the people involved. Three people being given a piece of blank paper and a pencil but no instructions as to what to do with them will probably have very different feelings about it. For example – panic (I don't know what to do, I'm no good at deciding, I can't think up good ideas, I know that whatever I do will be wrong); enthusiasm (I can do anything that I want, I've got loads of good ideas, I love the freedom of experimenting) or anxiety expressed as anger (How am I expected to know what she wants? What does she think I am – a mind-reader? She just wants to keep me quiet for a while. This is really boring). Panic and anger in situations such as this are often the manifestation of low self-esteem.

These three people may in the end produce three different pieces of work – one could write something, one could make a paper aeroplane and one could draw a picture. Events have significance in themselves but, perhaps more important, it is the way that we interpret them that determines our consequent actions and our view of ourselves.

13. My display cabinet (p.124)

This activity sheet highlights the difference between 'boasting' and celebrating the things and people that we are proud of or that we feel have been important enough to 'make a difference' to our lives. Children can fill in the sentences and add extra ideas of their own.

Important events may not necessarily be pleasant. It might be very important to one child that she fell and broke her leg for instance.

See notes for Activity 12 in this section and comments on pride and shame in notes for SILVER Activity Sheet 4 (p.62).

Expansion activities

(a) Read a story to the group about differences and similarities or self-discovery

For the younger age group I use *Something Else* by Kathryn Cave and Chris Riddell – a beautiful story about Something Else who tries to be like others but just isn't!

Another favourite is 'The House of Coloured Windows' by Margaret Mahy. This is a short story from *A Treasury of Stories for Eight Year Olds*. It tells of a girl whose greatest wish is to look through the coloured windows of a wizard's house. He tells her that she can choose the world that she likes best, but once she has chosen she must live there. Of course, from all the many different worlds she sees, she chooses to go back home.

Bill's New Frock by Anne Fine explores the differences between girls and boys. A funny and thought-provoking book for all ages, this can lead to excellent discussions with children about expectations, rules and children's views on how adults treat girls and boys.

Older children might also enjoy *Krindlekrax* by Philip Ridley. This is about a small boy called Ruskin who has knock knees, a squeaky voice and wears glasses. Will he get the part of 'hero' in the school play? The mysterious Krindlekrax gives Ruskin the opportunity to prove himself!

Daisy-Head Mayzie by Dr Seuss tells of a girl who suddenly grows a daisy from the top of her head and the various reactions of the people around her to this strange 'difference'. The daisy finally disappears, but the closing pages of the book hint at its occasional return (although it seems that Mayzie is becoming accustomed to it!).

(b) Take turns to tell the story of an important life event such as 'The day I started school', 'When I lost my front teeth', or 'When we moved house'

Providing the children with a theme which you know is familiar to most or all of the group is a good way to explore similarities and differences and is also very affirming for individual children. Youngsters love to hear stories about themselves and in small groups it is really worth spending time retelling these. For example, 'Yesterday Josh told us this story... One day Josh and his mum were in the park and...'

Vivian Paley is an ardent advocate of storytelling in the classroom and I thoroughly recommend her book *The Boy who would be a Helicopter* as an inspirational look at how this works with troubled children.

(c) Make up a story about a magic mirror

This can be done individually, or each child in the group can add to the story in turn. If the children are willing to share their stories then I suggest that you create a special time for this at regular intervals. Cover a chair with a special cloth, dim the lights and invite each child to sit in the 'storyteller's chair'. A joint story could similarly be written out and read aloud by one or two of the children.

(d) Take turns to re-tell favourite fairy tales or myths from memory

Traditional fairy tales and myths contain a wealth of images that represent unconscious processes. They can be a valuable tool in helping children to understand themselves and some of the dilemmas they face.

(e) **Make and decorate a large magic mirror. Each child has a turn on different days to have her photograph or drawing displayed in the mirror.**

(f) **Start a photo or self-portrait gallery of the group**

(g) **Set up a drama session where each child moves around the room as his or her chosen animal. See RUBIES Activity Sheet 2 (p.111). As the children pass they greet each other without using words.**

(h) **Have a display area where each child puts one special item or photograph that is important to him or her**

(i) **Have a 'bring a friend day' when each child brings a photo or drawing of a friend, family member or pet and tells the group about this 'friend'. See also the notes for EMERALDS Expansion Activity (e)**

(j) **Experiment with 'change'**

For example, everyone tries sitting somewhere different for a whole session, tries out a different hairstyle (even if it's just parting their hair in a different place) or wears something of a certain colour (you will need to have a ready supply of paper flowers, arm bands, etc. for those children who might forget or who don't have anything made of the chosen colour). Talk about how easy or difficult it was to make these changes.

(k) **Play the mirror game**

Children sit facing each other in pairs. They take it in turns silently and slowly to move their arms, hands, shoulders and head, while their partner tries to mirror their movements.

(l) **Spend time together researching RUBIES**

(m) **Use a confidence group for each child to take turns to tell the group one important fact about himself or herself**

References

Fransella, F. and Dalton, P. (1990) *Personal Construct Counselling in Action*. London: Sage.

Glouberman, D. (2003) *Life Choices, Life Changes: Develop Your Personal Vision with Imagework* (revised edition). London: Hodder and Stoughton.

Suggestions for further reading

Antidote (2003) *The Emotional Literacy Handbook. Promoting Whole-School Strategies*. London: David Fulton Publishers.

Bettelheim, B. (1978) *The Uses of Enchantment*. Harmondsworth: Penguin.

Dwivedi, K.N. (ed.) (1997) *The Therapeutic Use of Stories*. London and New York: Routledge.

Jennings, C. (1992) *Children as Story-Tellers. Developing Language Skills in the Classroom.* Melbourne: Oxford University Press.

Mellon, N. (2002) *Storytelling with Children.* Stroud: Hawthorn Press.

Murphy, C. (2000) *PSHE Through Fiction.* Cambridge: Cambridgeshire PSHE Service.

Paley, V.G. (1991) *The Boy who would be a Helicopter.* London: Harvard University Press.

Plummer, D. (2006) *The Adventures of the Little Tin Tortoise. A Self-Esteem Story with Activities for Teachers, Parents and Carers.* London: Jessica Kingsley Publishers.

Sunderland, M. (2000) *Using Story Telling as a Therapeutic Tool with Children.* Bicester: Speechmark Publishing Ltd.

Tyrrell, J. (2001) *The Power of Fantasy in Early Learning.* London and New York: Routledge.

Friends and Feelings (SILVER)

Aims of this section

- to further develop the use of imagework
- to explore the social skill of asking questions
- to explore and name a variety of feelings
- to understand more about the nature of feelings and how different feelings might lead to different ways of behaving
- to explore the nature of friendships

Additional materials

- card and safety pins for making badges
- coloured card for making friendship cards

Successful friendships are a powerful influence on a child's level of self-esteem and confidence.

> Stephanie (aged 11) was referred for therapy because of concerns over her moderate stutter. She made excellent progress until the point where she had to move to the next stage of her schooling. Her two best friends went to a different school. Her parents had initiated an appeal but unfortunately, for various reasons, Stephanie had to continue at her new school for several months.
>
> During this time her teachers tried to encourage friendships between Stephanie and some of her new classmates, but Stephanie's stutter became progressively worse and she became more and more withdrawn. She said that she had no friends and no one liked her. She began to somatise her feelings ('mistaking' an emotional ache for a physical one). She complained of stomach ache and sickness. Finally, Stephanie was able to change schools to be with her friends, and within a matter of days her speech had become markedly more fluent. Her parents reported that she was 'like a different child' – confident and happy and positively enjoying school!

Understanding relationships also involves understanding feelings. It is very self-affirming for children to realise that all feelings are valid and that they can have some control over the ways in which they express how they feel. Anger doesn't have to lead to physical aggression; feeling scared or anxious doesn't have to lead to avoidance; feeling excited doesn't always have to involve running around the room like a wild horse!

By valuing their own feelings and by facing difficult or confusing situations and coping with them successfully children will be able to confidently and creatively meet new challenges and develop their skills, so further strengthening their feelings of self-worth and self-efficacy. They will also develop a healthy level of 'emotional resilience': the ability to cope with temporary feelings of helplessness, frustration or upset without being engulfed by them or experiencing them as failure.

Activity worksheets

Introductory page (p.126)

I suggest reading this together with the children. Introductory pages are not intended to be used as an exercise in reading competency unless you specifically want to incorporate this into a planned lesson.

Facilitate a general discussion about friendships. Aim for the children to direct comments and questions to each other rather than through you. Allowing children to participate in collaborative discussion, rather than simple question-and-answer sessions, helps them to learn more readily and to develop a firmer level of self-esteem and a better understanding of social skills. For this to work well the children will need to have done preliminary work on group gelling and establishing group rules (see 'Working with a group', p.34). It may be useful for the group to recap on these 'rules' before starting the discussion.

1. Telling people about myself (p.127)

This exercise helps children to reflect on the activities that they did in the previous section and then moves them on to thinking more about how they interact with other people.

2. Finding out a bit more (p.128)

A chance to stretch the imagination again and to think about the social skill of asking questions. Talk about different types of question. Encourage open questions that would invite more detailed answers, rather than closed questions that might result in single word answers such as 'yes' or 'no'.

Try this out in role-play (see expansion activities).

3. Feelings (p.129)

See note for RUBIES Activity Sheet 2.

Children often find big changes or new situations difficult to handle and they need reassurance that this is perfectly normal and that we can do lots of things to help ourselves to cope.

To help children to think about this in more depth, discuss feelings of being in the group on the first day, their first day at school, first time in an after-school club, etc. Explore suggestions as to what made it OK or what might have made it easier (e.g. going with a friend, meeting the teacher beforehand, visiting the building and looking round, talking it over with a friend or adult, making a scrapbook to tell the 'story' of the changes being made).

4. How many feelings? (p.130)

Emotions tend to follow a developmental pattern and this should be borne in mind when working with younger children. Susan Harter suggests that shame and pride, for example, are not fully self-directed until around seven or eight years of age when children start to refer to feeling proud of themselves as opposed to referring to parents feeling proud of them: 'at this level, children appear to have internalized the standards by which shame and pride can be experienced in the absence of direct parental observation' (Harter 1999, p.106).

This emergence is, of course, partly dependant on parental modelling and cultural norms. There have been studies which suggest that self-directed shame may emerge at an earlier age in some cultures and that children who are constantly shamed may also internalise these feelings at a much earlier age.

Most children can name a few basic emotions with a little help to get them going. The more emotions that children can recognise and name, the more likely they are to be able to express what they are feeling without the need to show it by 'acting out' or by showing their feeling through a physical ache or pain. (Children may somatise feelings – 'mistake' an emotional ache for a physical one – because they don't know how to tell us what is worrying them or because they don't recognise the feeling.)

If children frequently deny or 'bottle up' their feelings then even pleasant emotions may eventually feel quite uncontrollable. If they are unaware of or afraid of what they feel then this will also affect how they interact with other people. For example, a child's first feeling after a difficult encounter with someone might be 'I feel bad' but he might express this as anger.

Useful, appropriate emotions brought about by realistic thoughts lead to positive action. For example, it may be appropriate for a child to feel anxious about some situations so that he can make sure that he is well prepared in advance or can choose not to enter that situation if the anxiety is well founded.

Stand in a circle and do a round of 'I feel_____'. Encourage each child to take turns to jump into the circle and show the group how he or she is feeling today (by physical posture and facial expression). Ask the rest of the group to copy the non-verbal aspects of this feeling so that the child in the centre can see what this looks like.

This activity, especially if done regularly, encourages children to recognise their own feelings and those of others and, one hopes, to come to understand that other people cannot *make* us feel anything. You might want to specifically make this point with older children.

It is also a great boost to self-esteem to have a feeling validated by watching others as they try to 'see how it feels'.

5. How I feel (p.131)

Children are often labelled according to their behaviour at an early age and they quickly absorb these labels into their belief system about themselves. If a child has always been told 'You're so grumpy all the time', then that is what he will believe and he is likely to act accordingly. Unfortunately, it is often the case that once this belief system is established, trying to change how a child views himself by telling him the opposite (in this case, perhaps, 'You seem very happy today') rarely works effectively. He will have to experience it often enough and think enough of himself for this to have an impact (see Part One, Chapter 1, p.15).

Choose some scenarios from the completed activity sheets and discuss whether other children in the group or class have been in a similar situation but felt something different.

Compare all the different things that lead to each child feeling excited or nervous.

Talk about how different people feel different things at different times. Talk about how feelings can change – what we might once have been nervous about we might eventually come to enjoy or to feel more confident about.

Point out any feelings that are similar in the group ('It sounds as though most people get excited when _____', 'Almost everyone feels nervous when _____', 'There are a few of us who feel disappointed when _____').

6. Imagining that feelings are colours (p.132)

Our moods change and that means that uncomfortable feelings, as well as nice feelings, will change, stop or fade away gradually.

Feelings could be explored as if they were different animals or sounds etc. but for this activity the children are invited to think about feelings as if they were colours. Talk about how we can feel like a different colour at different times on different days.

Talk about how two people could feel like the same colour for completely different reasons.

Help the children to elaborate on how they would move if they were being different colours. Invite two or more children at a time to move around the room as if they were being a certain feeling 'colour'. See if the rest of the group can correctly guess the colour.

Talk about how feelings can change very quickly, perhaps because of something that happens to us or something that we see or hear. Children can find it very hard to cope when their feelings change too frequently or too quickly. Brainstorm ideas for what we can do to keep our feelings more balanced. For example, if I keep getting angry I can:

- tell someone that I'm feeling angry
- sit and do a quiet activity until I feel more calm
- go and scribble in an 'angry book'
- write down all the things I'm angry about
- think about what I'm going to do later that I'm looking forward to
- daydream about the thing I'd like to happen that would mean I wasn't angry any more (wouldn't it be wonderful if I could have that new computer game/stay up late/go to the park; if I were invisible/a giant/an adult/I would _____!).

Of course, sometimes children don't know why they are feeling something. Acknowledging an unpleasant feeling can still help to dissipate it without the need to analyse it.

7. Teasing (p.133)

Very often children with low self-esteem are victims of teasing or bullying or they resort to being the teaser or bully themselves. Discussions about teasing are always lengthy in the groups I run. The intensity of focused concentration often needs to be relieved by an active game at the end.

Brainstorm different ways that people tease each other such as name-calling, taking and playing with treasured possessions, copying the way that someone walks or talks, consistently ignoring someone, and so on. Is there such a thing as OK teasing? At what point does having fun together become something that is not OK?

Brainstorm why people might tease – because they want to feel 'big', because they have been teased themselves, they've just been told off, they want to be part of a 'gang', they don't understand that what they are saying or doing is hurtful, etc.

8. Getting the picture (pp.134–135)

Read the exercise very slowly with plenty of pauses for the children to explore their images. As before, ask for verbal feedback when appropriate (see notes for EMERALDS Activity Sheet 1 and RUBIES Activity Sheet 2. Invite the children to talk about their images after they have drawn them. Compare and contrast the ideas. Point out similarities and differences in the images produced. As with all images, reinforce the idea that there are no right or wrong images, they all show different ways of looking at the problem.

9. More on teasing (p.136)

When you brainstorm 'what to do' be sure to accept all the contributions, even if you do not agree with some of them. Once you have collected all the ideas, talk about the consequences of each action. What would happen if you hit the person? What would happen if you told a grown-up? Children have often been told to 'ignore' the person who is teasing but I have never yet had a group where all the members agreed on this strategy. Many children tell me they've tried this 'but it doesn't work'. This might be because they need to come up with a *way* of ignoring, for example: 'I can name 30 different fruits in my head so that I can't hear what the person is saying' or 'I can turn and walk away and think about something nice that is going to happen at the weekend'.

Brainstorming the options and their consequences usually results in some useful ideas that children are more likely to try because they've come up with these solutions themselves.

> Michael (aged eight) suggested that he could stutter so much that he would get into the *Guinness Book of Records*; then he would become rich and famous, and the bullies would be really jealous! This led on to all sorts of other amazing ideas, but the group finally settled on a combination of telling an adult and saying something like 'I can stutter much better than you can' if anyone copied the way that they spoke. One child in the group still felt that he would risk the consequences and hit out, because that's what his dad had recommended!

10. All about my friend (p.137)

Important aspects can be written around or inside the frame, such as 'J. likes toffee' or 'J. is ace at mending things'.

11. Recipe for a good friend (p.138)

You can choose to be quite literal about this and have a potion of things like 'good at listening', 'good at sharing', 'fun', and so on (but see Activity Sheet 12 in this section).

Alternatively, this is a chance to explore the imagination even more and be wild and wacky with the potion ingredients! Christopher (aged seven), whose school report emphasised his limited imagination, put an iguana, mud, a frog and chocolate cake amongst his ingredients!

12. The House of Friendship (p.139)

This activity provides children with the chance to expand their vocabulary around the theme of friendships and to begin to think about the importance and the difficulties of friendships in more depth. Brainstorm this in the group first, and leave plenty of time for the children to fill in their own sheets with the words that are most important to them. Aim for a mixture of different aspects of friendships, including words that reflect some of the possible difficulties.

13. What makes a good friend? (p.140)

The aim here is to help children to think more about what a person can do to *form* friendships as well as to identify why it is that they get on with a particular friend.

Discuss the variety of answers that come up and lead this on to a discussion about having friends who are different from each other. For example, two very different children might be friends with a third child but not particularly close friends with each other. Encourage the children to think why that might be.

14. Special person for the day (p.141)

Make a Special Person badge. Children can take turns at being 'special' and have special privileges. It is best to have a random method of choosing children for this, such as putting names in unmarked envelopes or inside balloons and then popping one or more of the balloons at each session.

We usually have at least two special people each day when we run intensive courses for children who stutter. Their treats include extra biscuits and drinks at break times, being picked first for games and having a praise card designed and written by the rest of the group with at least six different praises on it.

Adam (aged eight) is a bouncy child with some mild language difficulties and a tense repetitive stutter. For a long time he has held the view that stuttering is his fault and that he should try harder to control it. He was accepted on a two-week course as it was felt that he would make more progress intensively than with weekly individual therapy. It was also felt that both he and his parents would benefit from meeting other children who stutter. Adam has a tendency to shout out and to jump around like a 'live wire'. Inevitably, he frequently drops things, bumps into people or says things that others find funny or irritating. He finds it extremely difficult to write legibly and tends to do everything in a rush. Adam insisted on praising everyone for 'using common sense'. This was not something we had talked about in the group at all. The therapists guessed that it might be something that he heard regularly from others.

His excitement over the possibility of being special person mounted as the days passed. On the second Monday of the course he told me that at the weekend he had slept with all his fingers crossed and was sure that today would be the day! Sure enough it was! He left the room (hugging himself!) while the rest of the group thought up praises for him. One of the older members pointed out that he might like to be praised for having common sense. This was duly written on Adam's card. When the card was completed and read out to Adam he couldn't stop grinning for the rest of the morning! I later overheard the same older boy praise Adam for being 'intelligent'.

The crowning glory was when Adam remarked to me that he not only thought he had done a particular activity sheet very sensibly and carefully (which was true) but also thought it was 'probably' OK to stutter a little bit.

15. My special friendship day (p.142)

See note for RUBIES Activity Sheet 9.

Discuss differences and similarities in people's ideas for their special day. Is there anything that could actually be incorporated into your self-esteem sessions?

16. Sharing (p.143)

Invite children to work in pairs for this one. Do a final discussion in the large group to bring together all the ideas. Focus on what makes sharing easy or hard and why sharing is important. Encourage a range of examples for things that can be shared (e.g. ideas, conversations, special moments, worries, secrets, friends, as well as perhaps more obvious things like games, sweets, toys, etc.). Talk about what to do or say when you really can't share something but you don't want to hurt a friend's feelings (how do you say 'no' to a genuine request without being aggressive?). See next activity.

17. When being a friend is difficult (pp.144–145)

This could be an appropriate point to talk about 'false friends' as well as about times when we have difficulties with good friends. Talk about making decisions about friendships based on facts *and* feelings. Talk about the idea of 'working things out' in friendships. Help the children to think specifically about the role they can play in working out disagreements.

See previous notes on 'looking back' at a situation (e.g. RUBIES Activity Sheet 9).

18. More than one (p.146)

See notes for EMERALDS Activity Sheet 1 and RUBIES Activity Sheet 2.

Before doing this activity, talk about the things that we can do to help groups to go well. Invite suggestions as to how different people might feel in a group and how feelings can change from the start of a group to the end of a group. Introduce the idea of endings – that if a particular group or friendship comes to an end that means that something new will be starting. Talk about the feelings that might be associated with this.

19. The magic mirror (p.147)

This doesn't have to be a self-portrait again. Children might choose to draw a picture of two people or a group playing together or talking together. They could draw something that represents what they feel when they are with friends. Encourage children to look back over the activity sheets they have done in this section and then to be creative in whatever they want to put in the mirror.

Expansion activities

(a) Read a story about friendships or sharing

For younger children I have used the following:

* *The Selfish Crocodile* by Faustin Charles and Michael Terry. This is the story of a crocodile that refuses to share the river with any other animals. He develops toothache but no animal will help him because they are too scared. A mouse dares to enter the crocodile's mouth, and all is resolved in the end.

* *Something Else* by Kathryn Cave and Chris Riddell (see p.56).

* *I Feel Bullied* by Jen Green and Mike Gordon (one of the 'Your Feelings' series).

Older children enjoy:

* *Friends and Brothers* by Dick King-Smith. A lengthier book, but it is worth lending it to children or reading out a chapter at a time as part of your planned session.

* *Skellig* by David Almond. This amazing story won the Carnegie Medal and Whitbread Children's Book of the Year. It is widely used as a Year 7 text but is also suitable for slightly younger children. David's little sister is very ill and he feels helpless. Then he finds a strange creature in the garage and he and his friend, Mina, carry it into the light. A book about forming close friendships and about support in stressful times.

* *The Angel of Nitshill Road* by Anne Fine deals with issues of friendship and bullying in a very positive way.

(b) Design an interview questionnaire together and ask each child either to interview one person in the group or to complete it as a 'do at home' activity. For example, they could ask questions such as 'How old are you?' 'What is your favourite TV programme?' 'What do you like doing after school?' and so on

(c) Draw pictures to express different feelings. These can be representative, such as a smiley face, or symbolic, such as a firework for excitement

Rachel (aged nine) drew pictures of how she felt when her talking was easy and how she felt when it was difficult. Her easy picture showed her sitting in an armchair on a high platform overlooking a green field. She gave it the title 'Enjoyable'. Her difficult speaking picture consisted of a red scribble with purple zigzags exploding from it. Her anger and frustration, clearly evident in the way she tackles her speech difficulty, were forcefully and very successfully expressed in this second picture.

(d) Make cards for friends

(e) Make up a co-operative poem or short story about friendships. Each person contributes one word or one sentence in turn. This works well if an adult acts as scribe and reads the composition to the group when it is completed

(f) Set up role-play situations – meeting someone for the first time; sorting out a friendly argument; dealing with teasing

(g) Write out several different feeling words on separate cards and several different activities (e.g. washing up, writing a letter). Children take it in turns to pick one card from each group and mime the combination (e.g. washing up angrily). The rest of the group try to guess what is happening

(h) Play 'Working Parts'. Small groups of children think of a machine that involves several working parts. They then work out a co-operative mime for the rest of the children to guess what machine they are being

(i) Use a confidence group for each child to say something complimentary about a friend or to say something about feelings

Reference

Harter, S. (1999) *The Construction of the Self*. New York: Guilford Press.

IV

Feeling OK About Being Me (GOLD)

Aims of this section

- to identify current strengths
- to begin to think about areas to build on
- to expand on the idea of skill-building
- to identify some of the elements that constitute a feeling of confidence
- to further explore the idea of accepting praise

Additional materials

- softball or beanbag for the circle game

Activity worksheets

Introductory page (p.149)

See previous notes on using introductory pages.

Encourage each child to say how he or she is feeling today.

1. Prize-giving day (p.150)

Many adults have told me that they would find this task very difficult! However, by this stage in the course most children will come up with plenty of ideas once they have been given a few pointers, such as: 'What about an award for making friends? Mending things? Playing football? Singing?' (See notes for RUBIES Activity 11.) This is usually also easier for them if the star system is already in place (see notes for STARS Activity Sheet 3).

Physical achievements are an important element in building and maintaining self-esteem for many children. A physical achievement might be something like climbing a tree, swimming two lengths of the pool, standing on one leg for one minute, running very fast. Children with restricted movement potential will also have important experiences of mastering physical skills which they can share with others.

Marcus (aged 12) was one of the children who could not think of anything that he had already achieved. He screwed up the activity sheet and threw it away. No amount of coaxing could persuade him to write anything on a new sheet. We eventually decided that every time he discovered something he would like an award for he could go back and add it to his list. This was a long process for him, but he did eventually find ten things. Occasionally he would ask me to confirm a thought – 'Do you think I'm any good at making friends?' – and we would try and think of concrete examples that showed that he was indeed 'good' at this.

I would like to add a note here about the use of the word 'good'. I believe that it should be used with care since it carries such a weighty opposite in most children's minds – if I am not good at something then I must be bad. The reason for the 'good' should be explained whenever possible. 'Good boy' is not really specific enough (I'm obviously being good but I'm not sure exactly what I've done). 'That's a good piece of work' is non-specific and potentially judgemental – what then is a 'bad' piece of work? Am I at risk of being bad or doing a bad piece of work without realising it? This is particularly relevant, of course, when a child has created something – remarks such as 'That's a good picture' or 'That's a good construction' or a 'good poem' are personal opinions rather than descriptions.

I try to encourage parents to avoid talking about periods of stuttering in terms such as 'He was really bad yesterday' but to think of it as something like 'It was a difficult day for him yesterday'. There are plenty of alternatives to 'good' and 'bad' that can be used instead. We cannot afford to underestimate the power of words and their contribution to a child's perceptions of himself (see also notes for STARS activity sheets).

Having discussed this at length with a student speech and language therapist I nevertheless found myself overusing 'good' in the very next therapy session that she observed. Changing habits takes time!

2. Loads of awards (p.151)

Children are more likely to experience increased feelings of self-efficacy if they spend time *talking* about achievements with others. Just having a list is not usually enough to validate them fully.

Each child could choose one of their achievements to tell to the group or to each other in pairs.

Talk about the different things that people like to get as awards. Many children will write that they got a new computer game or something else hugely expensive but in reality most are also very proud to receive certificates, medals, and so on.

As youngsters we rely heavily on external praise and rewards to help us to build self-esteem and a strong sense of who we are. It is not long, however, before we have to learn to internalise our praise. In other words, to recognise our own achievements and praise ourselves (see Part One, Chapter 2, p.21).

Encouraging children to look at things that they feel positive about is part of this process. For example, you can feel positive about your ability to run fast even without winning a medal for this!

3. Things I'm working on (p.152)

Children often think of 'things I'm working on' as 'things I can't do' or 'things I'm no good at'. Whenever appropriate, if you hear them using these phrases you might suggest that they feel what it's like to change the words to 'I'm working on ____'. If it's something that they are *not* working on because it simply isn't important to them (I personally don't need to learn how to change a car tyre because I no longer have a car), then rather than 'I'm no good at this' they could try 'I don't need to learn/practise this' or 'I have chosen not to work on this'. Watch out for the child who then uses this as an excuse for not working on something important!

Talk about how it is OK to make mistakes when we are learning things. When we make mistakes we find out how *not* to do things. This can sometimes help us to be more inventive in finding out successful ways to achieve our goals.

4. More awards (p.153)

See notes for Activity Sheet 2 in this section.

Emphasise that these awards are for all the effort that is needed when we are working on something that we find difficult.

Talk about all the different feelings that could be associated with being rewarded.

5. Star turn (p.154)

Initiate a round of 'I'm brilliant at ____' in the group. Discuss the variety of things that come up. If you feel it's appropriate you could talk about how people get to be brilliant at something. For example, this might involve discussion on learning 'sets' of skills and building up ability gradually. This can be compared to having a natural ability at something that might nevertheless need to be practised and developed (such as singing).

6. Confidence (p.155)

See also the notes on confidence groups (p44–47).

Confidence is quite a hard concept to grasp and yet most children with low self-esteem have the idea that they somehow need more of it. One way of exploring what confidence is all about is to think of someone who the children all agree *appears* very confident. This might be a TV personality or a fictional character or someone they all know. Make a list together of all the things that this person does which cause them to appear confident. Be as specific as possible. If someone says 'they *look* confident', then talk about how the person stands, walks, sits, dresses, their facial expression, etc. If they say 'they *sound* confident', talk about *how* they sound – Fast? Slow? Loud? Quiet? Somewhere in between? And so on.

The process of having identified some concrete things to do and ways to act will go some way towards helping children to create a feeling of confidence when needed.

7. Let's imagine (p.156)

This exercise uses imagework to explore confidence in more depth and to help children to begin to experience it in actuality, rather than just talking about it. See previous notes on imagework exercises (e.g. EMERALDS Activity Sheet 1 and RUBIES Activity Sheet 5).

Encourage discussion around the imagined animals that the children produced. For example, talk about the way that they imagined their CONFIDENT moved and felt. Relate this to how we can act in a confident way. Discuss the different points that children came up with relating to the positive things about being a CONFIDENT, also anything that they thought of that was not so helpful.

8. I felt confident (p.157)

Relate this exercise to previous discussions about feeling different things at different times. See SILVER Activity Sheets 3, 4, 5 and 6.

9. Praise (p.158)

See previous notes on praise, particularly the note on STARS Activity Sheet 3 and for Activity Sheets 1 and 2 in this section.

> Paul (aged ten) is a tall lad for his age and complains that he is often thought of as being older than he really is. He is expected to act in a 'grown-up' way and it seems that to a certain degree this includes being 'manly' in coping with emotions as well. When taking part in a praise circle in a group with ten other boys he showed us the qualities and characteristics that he perhaps really valued or wanted for himself when he praised others for being 'as gentle as a butterfly' and 'light and small'.

10. The magic mirror (p.159)

As before, this offers a chance to recap and decide on one aspect of this section to record with a drawing.

Expansion activities

(a) Read a story about confidence

There are plenty of children's books about confidence and feeling OK about yourself. These are some that I have used:

* *Scaredy Cat* by Anne Fine. Poppy is afraid of ghosts and monsters but needs to find a way of showing her classmates that she is not a 'scaredy-cat'.

* *Only a Show* by Anne Fine. Anna is worried about doing a five-minute show for her class. She is worried that she isn't confident, clever or funny and that she can't do anything 'special'. In the end, her show is a triumph.

* *I'm Scared* by Bel Mooney. A book exploring some of the things that young children are often afraid of. Kitty is afraid of the dark but she is able to come to the rescue when other children are afraid of things.

* *Fergus the Forgetful* by Margaret Ryan and Wendy Smith. Fergus can never remember things like taking his PE kit or his homework to school, but he is a mine of information about 'important' things and manages to help his school win a quiz.

* *Kiss the Dust* by Elizabeth Laird. Tara is a refugee from Iraq who is trying to adjust to a completely different life in England.

(b) Display pictures of 'things I'm brilliant at'. See if children can guess the owner of each picture

(c) Each child chooses a special word to describe herself, beginning with the first letter of her name (e.g. Energetic Erin, Smiley Sally). Stand in a circle and use a softball or beanbag to throw. On the first round the catcher says her own special name. On the second round the thrower calls out another child's special name as she throws the ball/beanbag to her

(d) Make lists of 'things I've learnt today' (not necessarily things learnt in the group)

(e) Display the confident pictures the children drew in Activity 7. Talk about the opposite of being confident. Draw pictures to represent this opposite

(f) Make collaborative pictures to show ways of praising or to show achievements

Join several large sheets of paper so that groups of children can sit round in a circle or square to add their bit. This is a good exercise in co-operation and in trying to see things from another person's perspective. The children will need to decide which way up the picture is going to be, how best to divide up the space, whether they will allow any overlap of pictures, and so on. For older children, this can form a good basis for discussion on maintaining group co-operation.

V

Taking Care of Myself (PEARLS)

Aims of this section

- to help children to identify their own self-help resources
- to introduce the idea of needing to prepare for difficult challenges
- to help children to be aware of the physical feelings associated with anxiety and how they can have some control over these
- to encourage self-monitoring of feelings and thoughts
- to encourage identification of worries and concerns and to show children that they can develop successful ways of dealing with these

Additional materials

- a box to decorate and post worries into (Activity Sheet 12)

Activity worksheets

Introductory page (p.161)

Compare and contrast 'taking care' while doing something (such as school work) and looking after ourselves.

Take time for a brief recap of the treasure that has already been collected.

1. Prepare to dive! (p.162)

I originally had the symbol of going mountain climbing for this activity sheet but eventually decided that I have personally done a fair bit of that (metaphorically, not literally!) and would rather use a symbol of diving. The idea of finding pearls, albeit amongst wrecks and seaweed, really appeals to me!

If a child was going to enter a sports competition or go on an arduous mountain trek they would need to be properly prepared and would be supported and encouraged to take time to build their strength, skills and stamina beforehand. Yet how often are children faced with stressful situations in daily life feeling unprepared or unable to cope with the unknown? This exercise can be used as a starting point for discussion on the importance of preparing for new or difficult things.

2. Feelings (p.163)

The interaction between mind and body has been studied extensively (see Part One) We know that the mind and the body are in constant communication with each other as different 'systems' of the body respond to messages from the mind and vice versa. The imagination has an important part to play in this process.

For example, worrying about (or getting excited about) an event long before it happens or even after it has already happened, can cause the body to react as though the event were actually happening now.

THE STRESS REACTION

There are several ways in which too much stress can upset a person's well-being. There are also many normal reactions that occur when we are faced with a stressful situation. These reactions prepare the body for 'flight or fight', in other words to enable us to physically fight the oncoming threat or to run away from it. If the reaction is completed and the 'danger' is dealt with, then the body can relax again. Unfortunately, we often produce the fight/flight reaction in situations that don't actually need a physical response. This may occur when children are concerned about such things as a forthcoming test, a potentially difficult conversation, being in the school play or being late for a school trip. Unwanted stress reactions can also occur when the original stressful situation is no longer there but we have not done anything to ease the stress response.

A threat to self-esteem can sometimes have the same physical effects as if you were actually in some sort of danger and preparing to fight or run away. Negative self-talk tends to prolong the stress response because if you tell yourself such things as 'I can't cope; it's all going wrong' your body continues to react by staying ready for action.

Young children, particularly those who have already experienced many stressful situations as babies, can find self-regulation of emotions extremely difficult. This is partly due to the level of neuronal development and to chemical changes in the brain. The ability to regulate emotions is also shaped by experience. To begin with, adults therefore need to support such children by providing reassurance and acting as an appropriate role model. Children also need to have some understanding of how physical feelings and thoughts and emotions are linked. You could explain this in terms of eating healthy food and junk food. For example, when we think thoughts like 'I'm hopeless', 'I can't do this' or 'No one will speak to me', this is like eating junk food – these thoughts affect our body in a negative way. When we have thoughts like 'I can learn how to do this' or 'This might be difficult but I'm going to have a go', 'It doesn't matter if I make a mistake so long as I try my best' or 'I know how to be a good friend' then this is like eating healthy food and these thoughts are good for us.

3. Feeling tense (p.164)

See previous notes on imagework (e.g. EMERALDS Activity Sheet 1 and RUBIES Activity Sheet 2).

Body awareness is an important factor in helping children to understand their emotions. By being aware of how they are physically experiencing their emotions they will also be more aware that they have some choice about controlling these feelings.

This activity should be done in conjunction with Activity 4 so that children can feel the difference between being tense and being relaxed. Relate this to Activity Sheet 2 as well and reinforce the idea that we can sometimes change the way that we feel physically in order to have an effect on how we feel emotionally.

4. Feeling relaxed (p.165)

See previous notes on imagework.

I usually use this activity sheet after actually doing a relaxation with the children. Learning to relax the mind and body is a skill that needs to be practised regularly in order to reap its long-term benefits. Even the most tense-looking children eventually learn to let go of unnecessary muscle tension during relaxation sessions.

I tend not to use the progressive relaxation methods very often (tensing then relaxing different muscle groups) as I find that some children tense up so much they find it hard to let go again! Mostly I use a method of focusing on different parts of the body and letting relaxation happen at its own pace (see Appendix B). Sometimes I use music or storytelling to facilitate this.

You may have your own favourite method of relaxation to use, but it is worth experimenting with different types over a few sessions and asking for feedback from the children as to which one they found most helpful.

If any children want to (they usually do!), then take time to share the imagework pictures of being tense and being relaxed. Point out some similarities and differences between different children's pictures and also between the images produced by individual children.

Talk about the different physical sensations that we produce in our body when we are relaxed. Spend time thinking of as many words as you can to describe what it's like to feel tense and relaxed.

> Laura (aged ten), who at first told me she couldn't draw, produced a picture of herself lying on a sun lounger beneath a palm tree. Matthew (aged nine) drew his cat curled up in front of the fire at home. Simon (aged nine) drew a sunset. All very different. All expressing the feeling of relaxation.

5. *Growing happy feelings (p.166)*

Discuss the different ideas that the children come up with. Celebrate the differences!

6. *Relaxed breathing (p.167)*

Take some time to look at pictures of the lungs and trachea (windpipe). This may seem a bit technical after the imagework sessions. However, I believe that it is useful to demystify the workings of the body so that children can realise that they have the ability to change their automatic reactions to stress and anxiety when these are not helpful to them.

The missing words are:

- lungs
- oxygen
- in
- out
- out
- lungs
- in
- lungs

Do a 'calm breathing' exercise (Appendix C).

7. *An image for calm breathing (p.168)*

See previous notes on imagework (e.g. EMERALDS Activity Sheet 1 and RUBIES Activity Sheet 2).

8. *Taking care of myself every day (p.169)*

Contrast different ways in which people (children *and* adults) choose to relax. Highlight the need to unwind in some way when things have been very busy. Talk about mental and emotional 'busyness' as well as physical 'busyness'. Discuss the importance of physical activity as being one way to relax the mind.

9. *How to make a perfect day (p.170)*

Encourage fantastical answers again. Giving children their wishes in fantasy can be a great way of relieving pent-up frustration (see notes for Activity 11 in this section and Parent Information Sheet 3B in Part Four, p.248).

10. *Letting go of worries (p.171)*

Worry involves thinking about, talking about and imagining what we *don't* want to happen in life. You will probably have been aware that during long periods of worry your body reacts as though the event is actually taking place now. Most noticeably, your muscles will tense ready for action. Worrying can wear us down and sometimes leave little room for other thoughts. Writing a worry down or telling someone else often helps to lessen it.

Sometimes, if worries can't be dealt with straight away, they do at least need to be deposited or offloaded somewhere. The HugMe tree is designed to be just such a place (but it needs a hug afterwards!).

This idea could also be extended to having a fruit tree – a tree that can have apples or pears or exotic fruit hanging from it, each marked with an achievement or something that children like about themselves, or perhaps compliments that they could 'pick' to give to someone else.

11. Any more worries? (p.172)

Facilitate a discussion about what could happen to the worries. Encourage fantasy solutions as well as more practical ones. For example:

> They should be tied up in a bundle and sent to _____ who would read each one and discuss them with _____. Laws would be passed to make _____ illegal. Everyone who had ever worried about _____ would receive _____. All the worries would then be _____.

Make a brightly coloured 'worry box' and invite children to post any worries that they may have. Set aside a particular time, perhaps once a week, to check the worry box with the children and problem-solve any worries that are there.

The worry box is always well used in our therapy groups. Because the worries will be read out it is, of course, important to tell the children beforehand that these will be brainstormed in the group (they can be posted anonymously). I know that some schools already use this idea and one of the things to be aware of here is that teachers or therapists may find some worries posted that would need to be taken further because they potentially involve others.

In our groups, worries tend to centre quite naturally on speech and language difficulties and feelings of anxiety when speaking. There was once a worry about nightmares posted and the group came up with some excellent suggestions for dealing with this. Once the worry has been resolved, or the child feels that he or she is coping with it, then the piece of paper can be ceremoniously torn up or put through the shredder.

> Craig (aged seven) was having a tough time at school because he was finding 'everything too hard'. He began to cry every morning and to plead with his mother to keep him at home. Craig and I wrote an 'I hate school because' list outlining all his worries. We made two versions – one for him to talk about with his mother and one to go in the worry box – with each worry on a separate slip of paper. In fact, unasked, Craig rewrote his list at home and decorated it. His mother took it to school and discussed the contents with the head teacher. Within days the worries had been mostly addressed and Craig

had stopped crying in the mornings. On his next visit to see me he asked if we could tear up all the worries except one that hadn't been 'fixed' yet!

12. The worry team (p.173)

Facilitate a discussion about what could happen to worries. Ask questions such as: 'What would you like your worries to do? Imagine this happening. What happens next? Then what happens?'

For example, worries can disappear, grow bigger, shrink or change into something else. We could make friends with them, throw them away, send them to the moon, or take them to 'obedience' classes!

Talk about different types of worry. Is there such a thing as a 'useful' worry? What would life be like if we never had any worries?

13. The magic mirror (p.174)

See previous notes on using the magic mirror.

Expansion activities

(a) Read a story about worries or a story about a perfect day

My books about worries became well worn very quickly! I like the classic Dr Seuss book *I Had Trouble in Getting to Solla Sollew* – a 'fable' about facing up to your troubles. Also popular amongst the children (and, I have to say, amongst many of my colleagues!) is *The Huge Bag of Worries* by Virginia Ironside. Wonderfully illustrated by Frank Rodgers, this is the story of a young girl whose bag of worries gets bigger and bigger and no one seems to be able to help until the old lady from next door suggests something radical – open it up and show the worries some daylight!

The Brave Little Grork by award-winning Kathryn Cave is a lovely story for the younger age group. Illustrated by Nick Maland, this is a story about the value of friendship and overcoming childhood worries.

I have also used *I'm Worried* by Brian Moses, one of the 'Your Feelings' series. This contains notes for parents and teachers with lots of suggestions for group activities and discussions. Further reading books are listed at the end of the book, and the author writes that the activities will 'satisfy a number of attainment targets in the National Curriculum Guidelines for English at Key Stage 1'.

(b) Outline different situations and talk about what children might specifically do, using ideas from all the activity sheets completed

I usually suggest that children come up with at least three things that they can do for each situation. For example:

* When x happens I will _____, _____, or _____
* When I notice myself getting uptight/feeling cross I will _____
* When I feel happy I will _____

(c) Take turns to say something nice that's happened today even if it's 'I had a tasty breakfast'

(d) Make a worry box and problem-solve any worries that find their way into it

(e) Do a relaxation session and tape it so that individual children can use this on a regular basis

(f) Make a giant paper HugMe tree to put on the wall. This can be used to hang up worries or 'Things I'm proud of'

(g) Make up group or individual stories about worries, e.g. 'The Day the Worries Took Over Our School!'

VI

More Than Just Talking (SAPPHIRES)

Aims of this section

- to identify the various elements that contribute to successful communication
- to help children to identify their own strengths and areas to work on with regard to communication
- to explore the variety of ways in which we express ourselves

Additional materials

No additional materials are required for this section.

Activity worksheets

Introductory page (p.176)

This could be used in a speech and language therapy group to promote discussion about various things that can happen to someone's speech. Even in a non-therapy group it is helpful for children to discuss this, although perhaps not in as much detail. It heightens awareness of natural differences and also of the fact that many people get anxious about speaking at times, whether or not they have a specific speech difficulty.

1. All about how we talk (p.177)

Speech and language therapists may want to discuss this in depth. Again, it is useful for any group to explore how we speak in order to help children to be more tolerant of differences, and also more tolerant of their own natural mistakes.

2. Conversations (p.178)

An activity sheet to encourage children to think about wider issues other than just speech.

Talk about the wide variety of different types of conversation – with one other person, in groups, about something serious, during play, about something familiar, about something new, and so on.

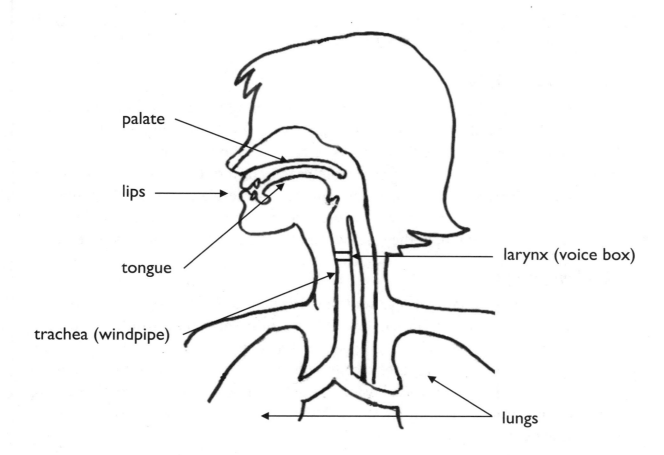

palate

lips

tongue

trachea (windpipe)

larynx (voice box)

lungs

3. Talking skills (p.179)

Children might just give quick, unconsidered answers to the four specific questions on this activity sheet. To encourage a much wider range of ideas, brainstorm in the large group if you feel it is necessary.

4. Listening skills (p.180)

An activity sheet to encourage children to think about listening as a skill which requires some focusing of attention. Talk about how we can sometimes hear several things at the same time (e.g. the television, someone talking and the phone ringing), but we can choose which one to actually listen to.

5. Let's imagine (pp.181–182)

There are several possible areas for discussion arising from this activity sheet. For example, a key social skill is knowing how to start a conversation in a natural relaxed way. Different people will have different ways of doing this and there really are no hard and fast rules but there are some general guidelines which can help children to get started.

Use a role-play situation engineered between two adults if you think your group would pick out the important social skills, or lack of them, by watching and listening rather than from a story.

Discuss the alternative, more successful scenario, demonstrating social skills if needed.

6. Taking turns (p.183)

Relate your discussion to a variety of activities that require turn-taking if they are to work well. For example: team games; a joint storytelling; board games; as well as conversations. Demonstrate a conversation with another adult where turn-taking is not used and compare this to a conversation where you both take more or less equal turns. Encourage children to role-play this in small groups.

This activity sheet can also be used to give children with a speech difficulty the chance to say how they feel when others don't give them time to talk.

7. Looking (p.184)

Maintaining appropriate eye contact is one indicator of feeling comfortable in a situation. When a child has low self-esteem he may find it difficult to keep relaxed eye contact with certain people. It may feel as though the other person can 'see' his true thoughts or recognise how ill at ease he is if he allows them to look directly into his eyes. Losing eye contact is also a way of avoiding seeing any possibly unpleasant facial expressions in response to what he is saying or how he is saying it.

You will need to be aware of any cultural issues related to this. For example, it may not be appropriate for some children to use prolonged eye contact with certain adults.

8. Keeping good eye contact (p.185)

Ideas might include talking for one minute on a chosen topic whilst trying to look at everyone in the group at least once; watching a video or TV programme and observing the level of eye contact for different speakers and listeners. (See also the discussion of confidence groups on p.44–47).

9. Body talk (p.186)

Talk about how we can show the same feeling in lots of different ways. For example, ask the children how they show that they are excited. Some children may be very active when they are excited, some may use an 'excited' gesture like clapping their hands, and some may just smile or laugh.

Discuss the idea that we could show different emotions in almost the same way (e.g. a child could cry because he's sad or because he's angry) and we have to look for other clues to help us to know what the feeling really might be.

Act out different emotions and see if the children can guess how you are feeling. Talk about both obvious body language and more subtle things, such as looking away.

10. *How do we sound when we talk? (p.187)*

This exercise helps to highlight differences and similarities in how people talk. For therapy with children who have particular speech difficulties it could lead on to more specific discussion about what can go wrong with speech.

11. *Speaking in a group (p.188)*

Compare and contrast groups of various sizes and who might be in each group. Do different children have different perspectives about groups?

Discuss what can be done to help the person who is talking (listen, sit still, keep good eye contact, smile, ask questions, etc.). See the notes on confidence groups on pp.44–45.

12. *What I feel about speaking in a group (p.189)*

Talk about what helps and what hinders. Help the children to problem-solve wherever possible.

13. *Talking time (p.190)*

It is helpful for children to understand not only that it is easier for us to talk about important things at certain times but also that it is easier for others to *listen* at certain times. This helps them to see that sometimes people may not be able to listen fully because of circumstances rather than because of dislike or rejection of the child or what he has to say.

Examples of easy and difficult times might be:

It's easy when...	*It's harder when...*
Mum and I are having tea together	We are rushing to get to school
I'm happy/relaxed	I'm angry/tired/upset/very excited
I'm with my best friend	Dad is watching TV
The other person is listening well	Everyone is talking at the same time
I'm in a small group	I'm in a big group
I know everyone	I don't know everyone

14. *What I like about the way I talk (p.191)*

This is an exercise in recapping on the section and formulating a clear picture of successful communication skills, for example: I listened, I took turns, I asked questions, and so on. This is the list of dos and don'ts that one group of

9–11-year-olds came up with when asked to produce an information video about talking skills:

- Don't change the subject.
- Don't be distracted.
- Keep good eye contact.
- Take turns; don't interrupt.
- Don't rush.
- Keep the right distance away. Not too close and not too far away from the other person.
- Talk loud enough.
- Listen carefully.
- Don't be boring.
- Ask the other person questions.
- Don't talk about something the other person is not interested in.
- Add to the conversation; make comments.
- Don't think about yourself all the time.
- Encourage the other person.

15. The magic mirror (p.192)

The picture the child draws in the mirror could be an image to represent a successful conversation. (The image that just came into my mind was the keyboard used to communicate with the aliens in *Close Encounters of the Third Kind*.)

Expansion activities

(a) Invite the children to move around the room greeting each other silently. Discuss different ways of starting and ending a conversation both verbally and silently

(b) Have whole conversations with no words. This is an enjoyable way to explore body language

(c) Each child tries a silent conversation between their left and right hand – an argument, a friendly discussion about what to do on Saturday, or one being happy and the other sad. Children then work in pairs to see if they can add spoken dialogue to each other's 'plays'. Volunteers show both versions to the group

(d) Take turns to give two-minute talks on any topic of the child's choice

(e) Watch part of a popular TV soap opera and pick out different examples of body language

(f) Problem-solve how to join a conversation as a late arrival to a group

(g) Play Chinese whispers and talk about listening skills

(h) Read a story about communication. I particularly like Nick Butterworth's *The Whisperer* – a book for young children about prejudice and diversity

VII

Solving Problems (RAINBOWS)

Aims of this section

- to help children to see that there are lots of different ways of solving problems
- to explore the idea that problems come in different sizes
- to help children to identify the problem-solving skills that they already have

Additional materials

No additional materials are required for this section.

Activity worksheets

Introductory page (p.194)

See previous notes for introductory pages.

1. Let's imagine (p.195)

Problems are different from worries (see earlier sections). Problems are tasks, dilemmas or puzzles that need to be solved.

Greg (aged seven) drew tigers to represent some of his problems to be solved. He decided that once they'd been sorted these problems would 'pop' and disappear.

Friend Max Callsme fatso

When friends don't Know about Nintendos

not many friends come Around my home

Brainstorm what to do for some common problems, e.g. you forget to take your lunch to school, your pet hamster gets out of its cage, you accidentally break something in school, someone borrows your pencils and keeps forgetting to give them back.

2a. A problem shared (p.196)

This exercise enables children to explore problems of their choice and perhaps put them more into perspective. Sometimes, as with worries, simply naming a problem and taking a good look at it can make it seem a lot less of a problem at all.

I have used all the activity sheets in this section with 'stutter' substituted for the word 'problem' in order to help children to explore their stuttered speech and the opposite of stuttering. 'Solving' a stutter appeals to a lot of children and they are very inventive in the images they use to depict stuttering and 'not stuttering' or 'relaxed talking', 'smooth speech' or whatever their opposite is. I recommend that only speech and language therapists try this in relation to stuttering, as you will need to know how to apply the children's images to actually helping them to maintain changes in their speech.

David (aged ten) was referred with a severe, tense stutter. He had attended several periods of therapy before we started to use imagery. David saw his stutter as a lion. It was, he told me, 'extremely big with a fluffy mane around its neck and a tail with a little bobble on the end'. Every time anyone went near the lion it roared and growled. When David became the lion and I asked him how he felt he said 'smug, happy and strong'. He said that the best thing about being this lion was that 'basically I can intimidate just about everything'. The worst thing, however, was that 'no one wants to be around me'. I asked the lion if he could see David standing nearby and if so, what did he look like? The lion said that David looked 'absolutely terrified'. He wanted to tell David to go away, but all he could do was roar and David just stood there. We spent some time swapping between David and the lion. David asked the lion to be friendly and to purr instead of roar. The lion was surprised that anyone would want to make friends with it! It could not promise only to purr but said that it would try to remember. David had no wish to change the lion in any other way. He acknowledged that it was there and still a lion.

David and I shared several imagery sessions together and did very little actual speech control work. His stutter became progressively less tense, until he eventually had several weeks at a time when it had virtually disappeared.

2b. Problem talk (p.197)

See previous activity sheet 'A problem shared'.

2c. Where has it gone? (p.198)

See previous two activity sheets.

2d. Something changes (p.199)

Solutions are often not the opposite of the problem, nor are they halfway in between. More usually, they require elements of both ends of the spectrum, producing something new – an inspirational idea!

2e. Making it happen (p.200)

It is important to actualise the images – to identify what steps could in fact be taken to initiate the desired change. Even the act of identifying the steps can start the process going at some level.

3. One less problem (p.201)

Encourage recognition of previous experiences of problem-solving. It is helpful if children can realise that each time they solve a problem, they are creating new possibilities for themselves.

4. Still puzzled? (p.202)

This activity sheet has been added at this point because so many children are reluctant or even afraid to ask for help when they need it. They may feel that this is further evidence that they are failing and may therefore use other strategies, such as watching other children and following their lead, or perhaps waiting passively until someone *offers* help. Feeling that it is OK to ask someone to repeat an instruction or that it is OK to say 'I don't understand' is a big step for many children with low self-esteem. Brainstorming this in a very 'matter of fact' way can help them to feel that it is a natural part of the learning process rather than a failure. Possible strategies might include:

- asking someone to explain it to me
- brainstorming it with other people in the group
- breaking the instruction down into smaller bits and doing one bit at a time
- asking for a repetition of the instruction/question.

5. A bit of magical wisdom (p.203)

I'm sure that most of us have had the experience of coming up with a solution to a difficult problem when we are least expecting it. We think about it for hours and come to no conclusions; so we give up and go for a walk, and suddenly the answer seems crystal clear! Or perhaps you have tried to think of a name or a song title but couldn't remember it, and then suddenly there it is just as you are falling asleep that night. Once again, naming the problem or defining the question can help to take some of the anxiety out of it. Often the child's innate wisdom will help them to solve it, even if that wisdom tells them to ask someone for help.

6. The magic mirror (p.204)

See previous notes on using the magic mirror.

Expansion activity

Read a story about solving problems

For young children you might like to use one of the following:

* *The Lighthouse Keeper's Lunch* by Ronda and David Armitage – a tale about how to foil hungry seagulls so that the lighthouse keeper gets his lunch.

* *Horton Hatches the Egg* by Dr Seuss. Horton is an elephant with a mission – to hatch the egg that a lazy bird has abandoned. He perseveres through all sorts of trials, including being teased by his friends, but he is triumphant in the end.

* *I Had Trouble in Getting to Solla Sollew* by Dr Seuss (also suggested for Section V 'Taking Care of Myself').

For older children *Hiding Out* by Elizabeth Laird is an excellent book about endurance and problem-solving. Peter and his family are on their way home from a holiday in France. His parents have an argument and in the confusion Peter gets left behind. He has no food or money but he finds a cave and the survival games that he had imagined become real.

VIII
Setting Goals (MOONBEAMS)

Aims of this section

- to introduce children to the idea of setting regular goals
- to expand on previous activities involving understanding the nature of change
- to provide a variety of ways in which children can monitor their own progress

Additional materials

No additional materials are required for this section.

Activity worksheets

Introductory page (p.206)

Talk about the sorts of targets or goals that people can set for themselves at school, with friends, in sport, in Scouts or Guides, etc.

Talk about individual targets and also group aims or goals.

1a. Taking off (p.207)

1b. Just the right star (p.208)

This activity is adapted from an original exercise by Dina Glouberman (Glouberman 2003, p.186). Projecting yourself into the future to imagine how things will turn out is a powerful aid to making changes. Such imagery requires the suspending of judgement and reality in order to act 'as if' you had already achieved some desired outcome.

Sometimes adults may encourage a child to try out new things that unfortunately then result in failure because the child has no motivation to change or no concept of how achieving the goal might affect how he feels about himself.

Imagery can provide a child with an opportunity to project himself forward in time in his imagination and see a positive outcome, experiencing it in his conscious mind and, in effect, creating a memory of the event as if it had already happened. This forward projection allows the child to recognise where he is at the moment – how far along the road he has already come – and to discover some of the things that he will need to know to achieve his goal. Perhaps other people will need to be involved, and the child can visualise how this might come about. He can also explore some of the things that might hold him back, things that he will have to overcome to achieve his goal.

It is important to help the children to identify particular goals before you start this exercise. I suggest that you then read these two pages to the group and ask for feedback as for the other imagery exercises. They will need to have paper and pencils near them in order to draw the star halfway through the exercise and to write a letter at the end.

If possible, it will be most effective if both these are done in silence without the children having to get up and move around to look for materials.

2. A letter to myself (p.209)

Once again, committing the thoughts to paper makes them more real. Dina Glouberman suggests sealing up the letter and sending it to the writer at a later date – a way of reminding them where they're headed.

3. Footsteps (p.210)

The ability to set realistic and yet challenging goals is an important but often undervalued skill.

A child who sets herself goals and is ready and able to evaluate her own progress on an ongoing basis will find that she has a clearer sense of direction and purpose and can accomplish more in a short period. A sense of control leads to higher self-esteem, which is more likely to result in higher achievements.

Many children do not set themselves goals because they have had past experience of failure, or because they have heard too often that they will not be able to achieve them. The idea that this is now true ('I never manage to do what I really want') becomes their own self-limiting belief. Children usually need help to set realistic goals without being overly ambitious. We can encourage them to be clear about what they are aiming for and to recognise the benefits of achieving the goal by looking at the smaller steps that they need to take along the way.

4. If I were famous (p.211)

This activity is another way of identifying long-term goals. It could be done as a newspaper article: think up the headline first and then fill in the details, being as descriptive and precise as possible.

5. Recipe for success (p.212)

This exercise is best done as a brainstorm first and then children can pick out individual ideas that they think would be right for them.

6. My treasure chest (p.213)

Talk about the different treasure that the children choose. Make regular times when children can 'find' something in their treasure chest to share with the group.

7. Goal record sheet (p.214)

The ability to self-evaluate is a difficult skill for children with low self-esteem. They may need to try several different methods and talk over their goal record sheets with an adult and with each other so that they get used to setting their own goals and knowing how to move on to the next step.

Facilitate a discussion about 'change'. In particular, encourage children to think about the following:

Why would someone change? For example:

- Because they want to feel better.
- Because someone else suggests it.
- Because they think they should.
- Because they want to be like their friends.

What do we need to have or to know in order to change? For example:

- We need to know what the change will involve.
- We may need help from others.
- We need to really want the change to work for us.

What makes change easier to cope with? For example:

- When there are lots of people making the same change.
- When we have already made a similar change so we can guess what it is going to be like.

What can we do to keep the change going? For example:

- Reward ourselves.
- Continue to set small goals.

These are just a few ideas to get things started. See also the expansion activities for 'Who Am I?' (RUBIES).

8. I can change the way that I feel about myself (p.215)

Help the children to identify a toolkit of things that they are going to do to keep up their confidence (or whatever their main goal is). They can then use this sheet to check off each achievement. The aim is also to help children to see that the skills and qualities they already have from other areas of life (such as perseverance and practice) can be put to good use when they are setting their goals. As each child has been working through the various activity sheets, he will, one hopes, have identified the things that will be most helpful. A possible list might be:

- I will reward myself when I have done well.
- I will take care of myself by doing something relaxing every day.
- I will answer at least one question in class every day.
- I will learn to swim.
- I will learn one new word every day.
- I will tell my teacher if I don't understand something.
- I will talk to my mum about my worries.
- I will make one new friend this term.

9. The magic mirror (p.216)

See previous notes on using the magic mirror.

Expansion activities

(a) If your group is coming to an end at this point it is important to prepare the children for this and have a final award ceremony of some sort

(b) Celebrate the completion of the activities book. Perhaps arrange a party and invite others to come and view the books and to ask the children questions

(c) Put on an end-of-course play, involving all the children

On intensive courses the children produce plays, depicting the archetypal hero's journey in which they meet their own images of confidence, wisdom, bravery and so on. In this hero's quest they are by no means the victim waiting to be transformed but are a proactive explorer rediscovering their own strengths.

(d) Jointly make a large cake with the word 'confidence' on it and share it in the group so that everyone has a 'slice of confidence'

Reference

Glouberman, D. (2003) *Life Choices, Life Changes: Develop Your Personal Vision with Imagework* (revised edition). London: Hodder and Stoughton.

Part Three

Activity Worksheets

This book belongs to

_____

Address

_____

_____

_____

Birthday

_____

STARS and EMERALDS

Getting Started

STARS

1. What are images?

Have you ever made up a story in your head? Imagined that you saw something that wasn't really there? Heard a noise and imagined that it was something scary? Have you ever remembered the taste or feel of something that isn't actually in front of you? Do you ever imagine that you are somewhere else or doing something different?

These are all images and they come from your *imagination*.

We all have the power of imagination and we can all use our imagination to help ourselves to sort out problems, feel good, cope with troubles when they come along and to help us to do the things that we want to do.

The rest of this book is full of ways for you to use your imagination in a helpful way.

2. Finding some magic

As you do all the activities in this book it will be like learning to be a magician. You will learn about the magic of your mind and you will learn a lot about yourself and about other people too.

Everyone has a little bit of magic treasure in them but sometimes we let it lie hidden or we forget that it's there.

The activities that you will do with your group leader or teacher will help you to find your own magic treasure. Maybe it's that part of you that feels confident and relaxed or that part of you that can learn more easily, or make good friends, or overcome a difficulty, or cope well with something that can't be changed.

Each part of the book has been given the name of something you could find in a magician's treasure chest so you will know when you have finished one bit and are ready to move on.

The first bit of treasure for you to collect is a handful of STARS.

3. My personal record of achievements

What does the word 'achievement' mean?

Use these stars to keep a record of all your achievements while you are working through this book. Can you think of one thing that you have achieved just a little while ago to write in the first star?

4. Things I would like to achieve:

_____

_____

_____

_____

_____

_____

_____

_____

Now let's collect some more treasure!

EMERALDS

1. Imagining

Let's check out what your imagination is like today. Ask someone to read the exercise 'Think of a chocolate cake' to you. While you are listening, imagine that you can see, hear, feel, taste and smell all the things that the person tells you about.

THINK OF A CHOCOLATE CAKE

Sit comfortably and close your eyes. Imagine that you are at home in the kitchen. Imagine that it is your birthday and someone has made you a huge great chocolate cake. It is in the fridge. You are allowed to go and get it.

Imagine yourself opening the fridge door. You see the cake on a big plate. What does it look like? You take it out of the fridge. What does the plate feel like? How do you carry the cake? What can you smell? You put the plate with the cake on it onto a table. Someone comes and cuts a big slice for you. What does this person say while they are cutting the cake?

What happens to the cake as this person starts to cut it? You reach out to take the piece of cake. What does it feel like when you touch it? Then you take a big bite. What can you taste? Can you smell anything? What do you imagine yourself saying?

Now let the images fade and, when you're ready, open your eyes.

See how good you are at imagining things!

2. Talking cats

Just imagine!

Imagine that you have a pet cat who can talk. This cat would like to know all the things that you do on school days. Make a list of everything that you have to remember to do. Start your list with 'I wake up'.

1 _____

2 _____

3 _____

4 _____

5 _____

6 _____

7 _____

8 _____

9 _____

You didn't have to wait until you had done each thing again before you wrote about it did you? You just *imagined* what you do each day.

3a. Becoming a cat

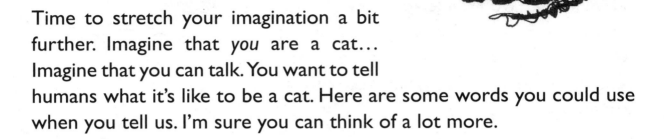

Let's imagine!

Time to stretch your imagination a bit further. Imagine that *you* are a cat... Imagine that you can talk. You want to tell humans what it's like to be a cat. Here are some words you could use when you tell us. I'm sure you can think of a lot more.

Describing words (adjectives)
warm   furry   soft   happy   sleepy   tired

Doing words (verbs)
purr   stretch   jump   climb   run   chase   stroke   eat drink

Naming words (nouns)
friend   basket   fish   milk

Close your eyes so that you can really begin to str–e–tch your imagination. Imagine yourself being a cat... Imagine what that feels like...

Ask someone to write down what you say while you are imagining that you are a cat. Think of a good cat name and then start with that.

3b. Being a cat

My name is _____

_____

_____

_____

_____

_____

Imagine that!

II

RUBIES

Who Am I?

Well done. Three emeralds collected so far and you've started to str–e–tch your imagination. Now you are going to collect a bagful of magic rubies while you find out a little more about being you!

Let's imagine that you have a magic mirror. Whenever you look into the mirror it will show you how you are getting along with collecting your magic treasure and learning about yourself and other people.

Start by drawing yourself as you are now. Or, if you like, you could paste on a photograph of yourself.

1. The magic mirror

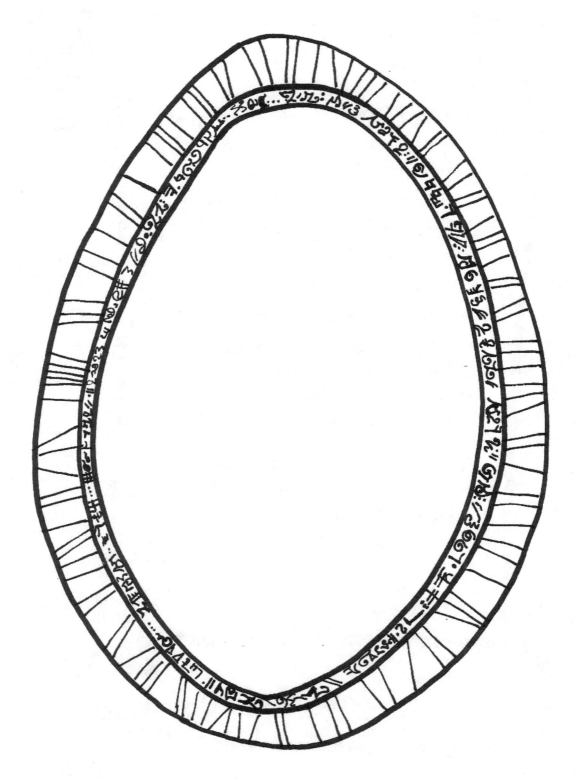

Look in the mirror and draw a picture of yourself.

2. If I were an animal

Close your eyes and take three deep breaths, letting the air out slowly as you breathe out…

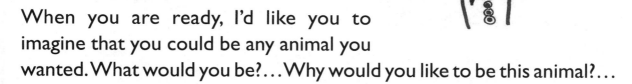

When you are ready, I'd like you to imagine that you could be any animal you wanted. What would you be?…Why would you like to be this animal?…

Imagine that you are this animal… Step into being this animal and really feel what that is like… Do you make a sound? What sounds do you make?… Do you move?… If so, how do you move?… Where do you live?… What do you like doing?… What do you not like doing?… What is the best thing about being you?… What is the worst thing?… What would you most like to be able to do?… What do you most wish for?…

When you are ready, open your eyes and draw or write about the animal that you chose on a large sheet of paper.

Imagine that!

3. Describing people

These are some words that I can use to describe people.

I can describe how they look (e.g. tall, short, blue eyes, curly hair):

_____   _____   _____

_____   _____   _____

_____   _____   _____

I can describe what they are like (e.g. happy, thoughtful):

_____   _____   _____

_____   _____   _____

_____   _____   _____

4. My group

Write down everyone's name in your class or group.

How do you think they would like to be described?

Write one friendly describing word next to each name.

5. This is me

Imagine that someone is writing about you for a newspaper. How would you like to be described?

The way I would like to be described is:

_____   _____   _____

_____   _____   _____

_____   _____   _____

_____   _____   _____

6. I am me

Imagine that you are your best friend talking about you. What would your friend say? For example, what might he or she say about what you like doing and what you are good at?

What might they say about what you *don't* like doing and about what worries you? Begin with your name:

_____ is _____

_____

_____

_____

_____

_____

_____

7. Everyone is different

Imagine what it would be like if each of us were exactly the same.

Imagine what your family would be like. What about your class or your street or town or the world?!

What would be one good thing about everyone being the same?

_____

_____

What would *not* be good about all being the same?

_____

_____

How are you different from one of your friends?

_____

_____

8. Something in common?

Sometimes you can find ways that people are similar. For example, people can be alike in the way that they look, how they behave, where they live, what they like to do or to eat and what they *don't* like.

Find someone in your class or group who is like you in some way. What is his or her name?

_____

How is this person like you?

_____

_____

Do you know someone who is like you in *lots* of ways? What is his or her name?

_____

How is he or she like you?

_____

_____

This is called 'having something in common'.

9. Making a change

Imagine that a magician could help you to change something about yourself. What would you want to change?

One thing I would like to change is:

Close your eyes and imagine that the change you wished for has already happened. How are you different? What is happening now? How do you feel? What will happen next? Draw or write about the change.

10. The change shop

Imagine a shop where you could buy, sell and change things about yourself.

Imagine what the shop would look like. Imagine the shop-keeper. What would you sell? What would you like to buy more of?

Draw or write about the shop here.

11. Things I like about me

Now think about all the things that you like about yourself and that you would not want to change.

Some things I really like about me are

_____

_____

_____

_____

_____

_____

_____

_____

12. Important people

Imagine that you are going to tell your class or group about all the people that are important to you.

What do you think the other children would like to know?

Draw a picture of one of your important people and write or draw about what he or she likes to do. Why do you think they like to do this?

13. My display cabinet

Imagine that you have a special place where you can put important things on show for everyone to see.

Think of some important things about you that you would want to put on display.

An important place for me is _____

A special fact about me is _____

An important day was when _____

My favourite food is _____

The thing I hate most is _____

An important person for me is _____

I would most like to _____

III

SILVER

Friends and Feelings

You have collected loads of rubies for your treasure chest. Well done!

Now we're going hunting for silver while we find out some important things about friends.

It's great to have friends. You can share ideas and worries with them. You can do things together like play computer games, go for walks or just sit and chat.

Sometimes friendships can be difficult too, like when a best friend moves to another town or when you argue about something or you both want to do different things.

Some people seem to make friends very easily but a lot of people find it hard to get to know others well enough to feel really comfortable with them.

With just a little bit of imagination the next part of this book will help you to find out more about friendships.

So – while you collect some silver, let's imagine…

1. Telling people about myself

Imagine that you meet someone for the first time. Think of three things that you could tell them about yourself.

_____

_____

_____

Imagine that you wanted to know about someone else. See if you can think of three things that you could ask them.

_____

_____

_____

2. Finding out a bit more

Let's imagine that you meet an alien! Think of three things that you would want to ask him.

_____

_____

_____

Now imagine that you are the alien. You don't know anything about earth or the people who live here.

See if you can think of three things that you would ask.

_____

_____

_____

3. Feelings

What do you think it would feel like to be an alien in a place that you didn't know?

Think of three words to describe how you would feel.

_____   _____

_____

What are some of the important things you would need to know?

_____

_____

_____

What else would help you to feel OK about being in a new place?

_____

_____

_____

4. How many feelings?

Part of getting to know people involves finding out how they are feeling. It is important to know about feelings. They are a big part of who we are.

There are lots of different words that *describe* how we feel. Here are just a few:

happy   sad   embarrassed   angry   excited

Write down as many feeling words as you can. Collect some more words from your friends and family by asking them how they are feeling.

_____   _____   _____

_____   _____   _____

_____   _____   _____

_____   _____   _____

_____   _____   _____

_____   _____   _____

5. How I feel

Having a feeling doesn't mean that you are always going to be like that.

Jenny might feel shy when she goes to a party where she doesn't know anyone but that doesn't mean that she is always 'a shy person'. There are lots of times when Jenny feels very confident.

Imagine some times when you have felt some of these feelings. Draw or write about each of the feelings listed on this page.

A time when I felt very brave was _____

I felt excited when _____

I felt relaxed when _____

I felt nervous when _____

I felt angry when_____

I felt happy when _____

I felt disappointed when _____

6. Imagining that feelings are colours

Simon and Jenny are best friends.

They both like to use their imagination. Sometimes they use their imaginations to help them to describe how they are feeling.

Today, Simon told Jenny that if he were a colour instead of a person then he would be the colour red because he feels very brave and strong.

Jenny said that yesterday she would have been red too because she felt very energetic, but today she would be blue because she feels very calm.

Imagine that you are a colour. Which colour would you be today?

If I were a colour I would be _____

Because _____

Imagine yourself *being* this colour. How do you move as this colour? Do you make a sound? If so, what sound do you make? What do you feel like as this colour?

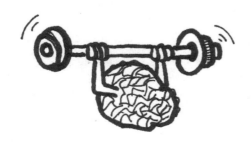

Now you are really giving your imagination a good workout!

7. Teasing

Let's spend a little time thinking about something that is not a friendly thing to do. Have you ever been teased?

What is teasing? Think of all the different ways that someone might tease another person.

_____

_____

_____

_____

Think about *why* people might tease.

_____

_____

_____

_____

8. Getting the picture

Let's carry on str—e—tch—ing our imaginations.

If you could get an image of what it's like to be someone who teases others and an image of what it's like to be teased that might help you to understand it even more. Ask your teacher or group leader to read 'teasing' to you.

TEASING

When you're feeling nice and relaxed invite an image to appear in your mind that somehow shows us what it's like to be a person who teases others. This image might be an animal, an object or a plant. Whatever comes into your mind first, let that be your image for a person who teases others…

When you have an image, spend a little bit of time finding out about it. What can you see when you look at it closely?… Does it move?… If so, how does it move?… Does it make any noise?…

Now imagine that you can become the image. Step into it…and see how it feels to *be* the image… As the image, ask yourself: 'What is the best thing about being me?… What is the worst thing?'…

If you could change something about yourself as this image what would you change?… What do you want to happen now?…

Gradually come back to being yourself again. Take a deep breath and step back into being you… Say goodbye to the image… Relax again…

When you are ready, allow another image to come to you that somehow shows what it's like to *be* teased…the first image that comes into your mind — it might be an object, a plant or an animal…

Getting the picture (continued)

When you have got an image spend some time finding out what it's like... Look at it from all sides...

If you want to, you can become the image for a while... Feel what it is like to *be* this image...

What is the best thing about being the image?... What is the worst thing?...

When you are ready, go back to being yourself again. Take a deep breath and step back into being you, just looking at the image.

Now look at both the images together... Imagine that you are an expert on the subject of teasing and what to do about it... Really feel how important it is to have this expert knowledge...

If you could give some advice to the two images, what would you say?...

If you could change something about them or about what is happening what would you change?...

Imagine that change happening and see what that is like... What do you want to say to the images now?... What do they want to say to you?...

When you have finished thank the images and say goodbye to them so that you are ready to *very* gradually come back to feeling more wide awake...and back in the room...feeling your feet touching the floor...and with your eyes open...

When you are ready, spend some time drawing or writing about what you imagined.

9. More on teasing

How does it feel to be teased? Think of as many words as you can to describe what people might feel like when they are teased.

_____   _____   _____

_____   _____   _____

Now let's think of some things that you could do.

If I was being teased I could

_____

_____

If I saw someone else being teased I would

_____

I would not

_____

10. All about my friend

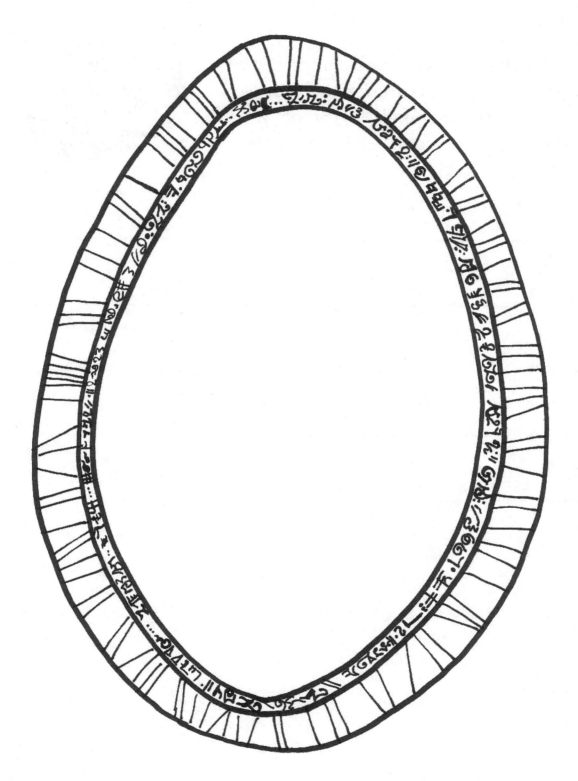

Imagine that one of your friends could look in the magic mirror. What would he or she see? What would your friend say was important about himself or herself? Draw a picture of your friend in the magic mirror.

11. Recipe for a good friend

Imagine that you have a book full of magic recipes. The very first recipe in the book is how to make friends. What do you think the magic potion will be made of?

_____   _____

_____   _____

_____   _____

_____   _____

_____   _____

12. The House of Friendship

Write down all the words about friendships that you can think of. Make sure you write some feeling words as well as some describing words. Write them on the House of Friendship.

13. What makes a good friend?

_____ is a good friend because

_____

_____

_____

Some things we like doing together are

_____

_____

_____

One of the nicest things I have ever done for a friend is

_____

_____

_____

14. Special person for the day

Imagine that it's your special friendship day.

Everyone is going to be extra friendly today. They want to know what you like friends to do so that they can be sure to get it right. What will you tell them?

 I like it when my friends

_____

_____

_____

 It is not friendly to

_____

_____

_____

15. My special friendship day

Imagine that it is the end of your special friendship day and you have had a wonderful time with everyone being extra specially friendly.

What did you do together? What did you do that helped the day to go well? What were you like with your friends? (For example, were you relaxed? Smiley?) How did you feel? What do you feel now? Close your eyes and just imagine…

When you are ready, draw or write about your special day here.

16. Sharing

What does the word 'sharing' mean?

_____

_____

Imagine that you've just had a birthday and you've been given some special pencils for drawing. You take them into school to use when you do your work. Would it be OK to share them or would that be difficult for you?

If I had some new coloured pencils it would be OK to share them if

_____

_____

It would be hard for me to share them if

_____

_____

What other things can be shared?

_____

_____

17. When being a friend is difficult

Let's say you and one of your friends disagree about something. Imagine that your friend has come to your house for tea. Your friend wants to play outside and you want to play indoors with a new game that someone has given to you. How does that feel? What might happen?

_____

_____

_____

_____

Imagine that it is time for your friend to go home now and you didn't manage to sort out the disagreement. How do you feel? What happened? What did you do? What didn't you do?

_____

_____

_____

_____

When being a friend is difficult (continued)

Now imagine that your friend is going home and you *did* manage to sort things out. You both feel OK. What happened? What did you do? What did you say?

_____

_____

_____

_____

_____

_____

_____

_____

18. More than one

You have had a lot of practice at using images so now let's imagine what it's like to be part of a group.

Close your eyes for a moment so that you can get an image (a plant, an object or an animal) that somehow shows us what a successful group is like.

When you have got your image I'd like you to imagine that you can *become* the image, just like when you imagined being a cat.

When you are this image ask yourself 'What is it that makes me work well?' and 'What is the best part of me?'

What do you like about being this image?

When you are ready, step out of being this image and back to being yourself... Let the image gradually fade...open your eyes... And draw or write about your image on a big piece of paper.

19. The magic mirror

Think about what you have learnt so far.

Look in the magic mirror. What do you see?

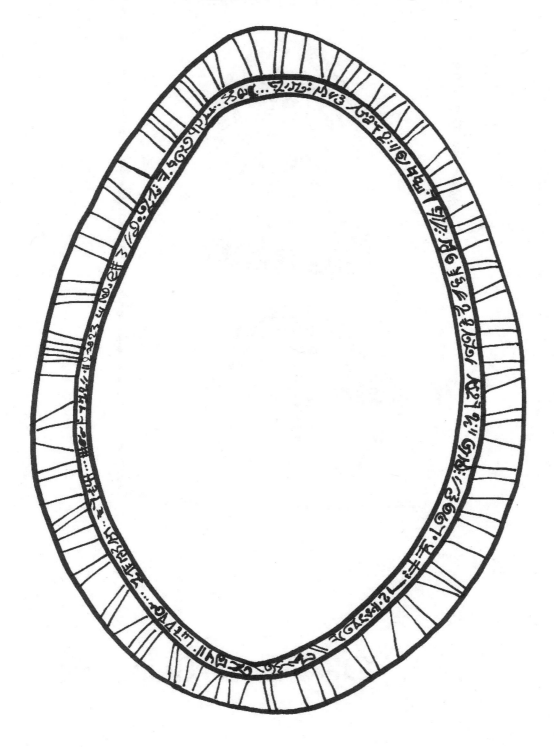

IV

GOLD

Feeling OK About Being Me

Lots of pieces of silver to add to your collection! Your magician's treasure chest is getting more and more full.

Now it's time to look for some gold.

Feeling good about who you are is really important.

There are lots of things that happen to us and around us that help us to feel OK about ourselves, but sometimes things happen that are not so nice and then we might end up feeling bad about ourselves.

We might start to think 'I can't do this' or 'I'm no good at this' or 'Everyone has more friends than me'.

If this happens then your imagination can help you to feel better about yourself again **AND** it can help you to actually get to *be* better at doing some of the hard things.

So – let's start collecting gold.

1. Prize-giving day

First of all, let's imagine that it is prize-giving day at the magician's school. Today you will be awarded for ten of the things that you have already achieved. Make a list of the ten things that you would like awards for and then write them in the points of the star.

2. Loads of awards

Imagine being in a big room with all the other apprentice magicians.

The chief magician calls out your name and reads out the list of your ten achievements.

Everyone claps as you go to receive your award. What do you get? How do you feel?

Draw or write about your prize-giving day here.

3. Things I'm working on

All through life we are learning new things and often getting better at some of the things we can already do or we already know about. Let's imagine that on prize-giving day at the school for magicians they also give awards for the things that you are working on.

These are the things that you know are a bit difficult for you at the moment so you are working on learning a bit more about them or practising regularly so they'll get easier for you.

Think of five things that you are working on and write them here.

4. More awards

Imagine yourself in the big room again with all the other apprentice magicians.

The chief magician calls your name and reads out your list of the five things you are working on. Everyone claps and cheers as you go up to fetch your award. What do you get? How do you feel?

Draw or write about it here.

5. Star turn

Now let's imagine that every person at the school for magicians gets a gold medal for something that they are *really brilliant* at.

What will your gold medal be for? Draw a picture or write about something that you are really brilliant at.

6. Confidence

What does the word 'confidence' mean?

_____

Some people can seem very confident. Most of us are confident in some things we do and in some places. We have to build up our confidence with other things.

Think about one thing that you would like to be able to do with more confidence.

I would like to be more confident when

_____

_____

_____

_____

7. Let's imagine

Imagine that CONFIDENT is the name of an animal.

It could be a real animal or a made-up one. What would it be? Can you picture it in your mind?

Now imagine that *you* are this animal. Step into being a CONFIDENT… Take your time and really feel what it is like to be this animal… What do you look like?… How do you move?… What noises do you make?…

What do you think about?… What are the nice things about being a CONFIDENT?… Is there anything that is not so nice?…

Where do you live?… Who are your friends?… What do you do best?… What is the most important thing about you?…

If you could give some advice to children about being a CONFIDENT what would you tell them?

When you have found out everything you can about being a CONFIDENT, come back to being you again… Thank your imagination for showing you this image… Let the image gradually fade away…

Remember that you can always call up the image again in the future if you want to remind yourself what it feels like to be as confident as this…

Come back to being in the room again…have a bit of a stretch and open your eyes…

When you are ready, draw or write about what it's like to be a CONFIDENT.

8. I felt confident

Now think of a time when you *have* felt confident. Draw or write about it here.

A time when I felt confident was

9. Praise

When someone has done something well or really tried hard with something they might be praised for it. The good thing about praise is that it can happen at any time and for *lots* of different reasons. We can praise other people and we can praise ourselves too.

To praise someone means

_____

I can praise people by

_____

When people praise me I feel

_____

Today I praised someone for

_____

Something I would like to be praised for is

_____

Today I praised myself for

_____

10. The magic mirror

Think about what you have learnt while you have been collecting gold.

Look in the magic mirror. What do you see?

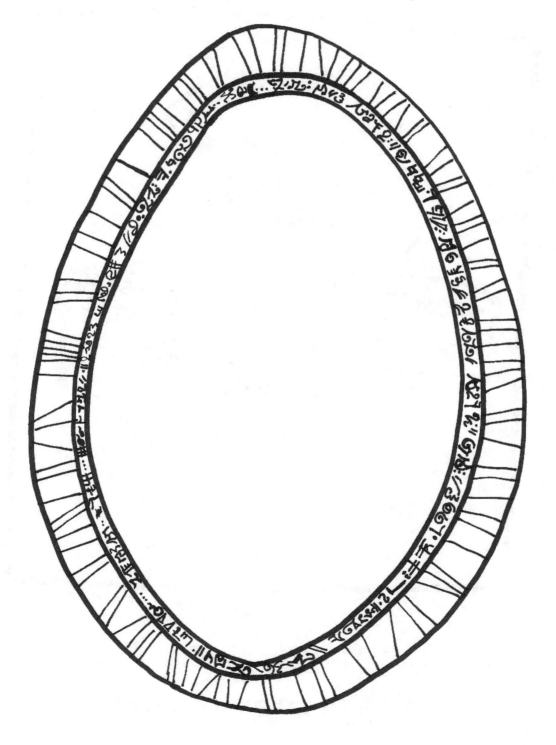

V

PEARLS

Taking Care of Myself

Lots of gold to add to your treasure chest! You're doing really well.

Now we will go diving for pearls.

With all these things to learn and friends to make and exciting things to do we'd better think about how we take care of ourselves and others.

There are lots of things you can do that will help you to look after yourself.

So – while you are collecting your pearls, let's imagine…

1. Prepare to dive!

When you look after yourself, you feel more ready to enjoy the easy, exciting or fun things in life and more ready to cope with those things that are especially difficult.

It's a bit like being ready to go diving in the sea.

Take a few minutes to think about what you would need to have with you and what you would need to know if you were going diving; in other words, how you would need to prepare.

Before I go diving I would need to be

_____

_____

I would need to have

_____

_____

I would need to know

_____

_____

2. Feelings

Have you ever worried about something that hasn't happened yet? What did your body feel like? Tick the feelings that you get when you are worried.

☐ butterflies in my tummy   ☐ heart beats faster

☐ headache   ☐ fidget a lot

☐ feel sick   ☐ can't think clearly

☐ tight muscles   ☐ wobbly knees

Have you ever got excited about something long before it happened? What did your body feel like then?

_____

_____

Your imagination can make your body feel different things. Sometimes this is good but sometimes this is not useful for you.

Sometimes you can change what you are imagining so that you can *feel* better.

Imagine that!

3. Feeling tense

Perhaps you have noticed that there are times when people might be feeling one thing but acting as though they are feeling something completely different.

Sometimes our feelings get all mixed up.

So let's think a bit more about what our bodies feel like when we have different emotions.

Think of a time when you felt a bit upset or cross about something. I bet your body felt very stiff and perhaps you felt a bit churned up inside? This is called tension.

If tension were an animal or a plant or anything else what would it be?...

Close your eyes and imagine something that somehow shows us what it's like to be tense...

Imagine that you can become your image of tension... Step into being this plant or animal or object... What do you feel like when you are this image?

What does your body feel like?... What is the worst thing about being this image?... Feel a frown growing from deep inside you... Feel it spreading all the way through you... Really notice what this is like...

Now step out of being this image and back to being you... Give yourself a shake all over...shake your hands, shake your arms, shake your body, shake your legs! Let all that tension disappear...

Draw or write about your image of tension on a big piece of paper.

4. Feeling relaxed

When we are not tense our body feels more relaxed.

If the feeling of relaxing was an animal, a plant or an object, what would it be?

Close your eyes and take three deep breaths, letting the air out slowly as you breathe out... Ask your imagination to come up with an image that somehow shows us what it's like to be relaxed... It could be an object, a plant or an animal... Whatever it is, just let the image appear...

When you are ready, imagine that you can become your image of relaxation...

Step into being this animal or plant or object and really feel what it's like...

What does your body feel like?...

Feel a smile grow from deep inside you... Feel it spreading all the way through you... Really notice what this is like...

What is the best thing about being this image?...

Spend some time just being this image and enjoying the feelings... When you are ready step out of this image and back to being you. Open your eyes slowly and have a stretch and a yawn!

On a large piece of paper, draw or write about your feelings of being relaxed.

5. Growing happy feelings

Let's imagine that you can grow happy feelings just like you can grow flowers.

Flowers usually need a lot of looking after to help them to be at their best.

Different flowers need different sorts of earth. Some like shade and some like lots of sun. Some will only grow where it is very watery and some like to be quite dry.

In the same way, different people would like different things to help them to grow happy feelings. Colour in the flower and write the things that *you* need for your happy feelings to grow.

6. Relaxed breathing

Imagine that your lungs are like balloons. They can get bigger when you fill them with air and then they get smaller again when you let some of the air out.

Sit upright in a chair and put one hand on your stomach. Feel what happens to your stomach when you breathe in and out.

When you think you know what relaxed breathing feels like, see if you can fill in the missing words below.

When I breathe, the air goes in and out of my l _ _ _ _.

I breath in air that is full of o _ _ _ _ _ and this helps to keep my body working well.

When I am relaxed and breathing easily my stomach goes _ _ and _ _ _ _.

When I breathe in my stomach moves _ _ _ because my _ _ _ _ _ _ are filling up with air.

When I breathe out my stomach goes _ _ because some of the air is going out of my _ _ _ _ _.

7. An image for calm breathing

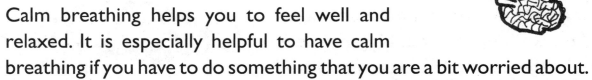

Calm breathing helps you to feel well and relaxed. It is especially helpful to have calm breathing if you have to do something that you are a bit worried about.

Doing some calm breathing before or after (or even *during*) a difficult time helps your body to relax once more. See if you can work your imagination again.

Imagine this...

Close your eyes and ask your imagination to come up with an image that somehow shows us what it's like to have calm breathing. It could be an image of an animal, a plant or an object. Whatever it is, just let it come into your mind.

Now look at the image very closely. Let your imagination look at it from the sides, from the back, from underneath and from the top (as though you are looking down at it). Take your time exploring the image of calm breathing.

Now see if you can *become* your image and really feel what it is like to be the image of calm breathing. Just imagine yourself stepping into your image and becoming it. Take a deep breath and let it go on a sigh. Now ask yourself 'What is the best thing about being this image?'... What can you do as this image?... If you can move, how do you move?... How do you feel now?...

Remember that whenever you are feeling a bit tense or worried, thinking of this image will help you to relax a little bit and to have the calm breathing that you need...

When you are ready, step back into being you. Thank your imagination for showing this to you... Let the image fade away... Gradually feel yourself coming back to the room...and open your eyes...so you are ready to draw or write about your image of calm breathing.

8. Taking care of myself every day

Imagine that you've had a very busy day at school and you feel quite tired.

Think of all the things that you could do now to help yourself to feel relaxed and refreshed. Draw or write about them here.

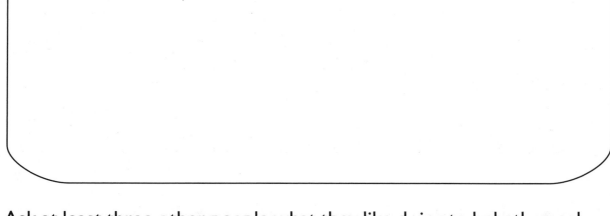

Ask at least three other people what they like doing to help themselves to relax. Write or draw their answers here.

9. How to make a perfect day

Let's go back to the magician's recipe book again and think about how to make a perfect day for ourselves.

What ingredients would you need for *your* perfect day?

_____   _____

_____   _____

_____   _____

_____   _____

Imagine that you have *had* the most perfect day. Describe what happened.

_____

_____

_____

10. Letting go of worries

Imagine that there is a tree called the HugMe tree. It is so big and has so many branches that it can take all your worries for you.

Draw or write about any worries you might have and hang them on the branches. You can use the HugMe tree at night to hang up your worries before you go to sleep. Just picture it in your mind.

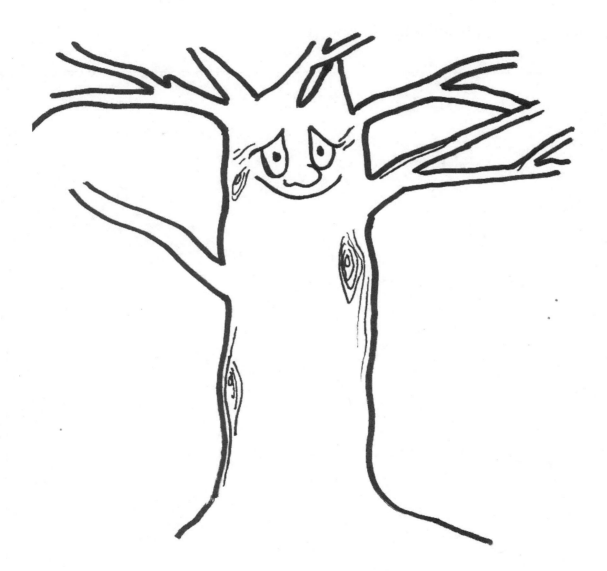

Imagine yourself giving the HugMe tree a great big hug!

11. Any more worries?

Imagine that you could post your worries into a worry box.

What do you think should happen to them then? Where would they go? Would anyone look at them? If so, who would it be? What would they do with them?

Draw or write about what happens.

Imagine that!

12. The worry team

Imagine that you are part of a worry team.

This is a group of exceptionally clever people who spend their time inventing ways of getting rid of worries.

They thought of the HugMe tree and the worry box. Make a list of other things that you could do with worries. How inventive can you be?

13. The magic mirror

Think about what you have learnt while you've been diving for pearls.

Look in the magic mirror. What do you see?

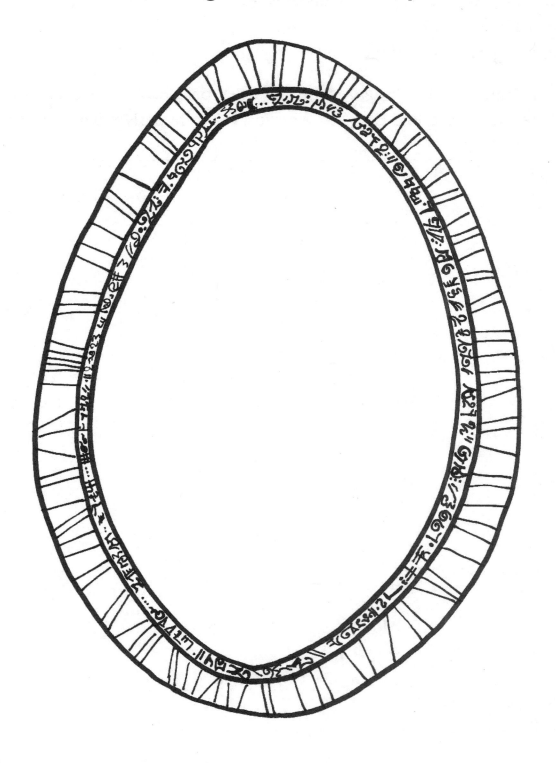

VI
SAPPHIRES

More Than Just Talking

Well, you seem to have things under control in the worry department! You have plenty of pearls brought up from the sea.

The next treasure to hunt for is a pocketful of sapphires.

Lots of people have difficulty with their talking. Perhaps you have some difficulty (like stuttering) or you know of someone else who does.

Even if you don't struggle with your speaking, perhaps there are times when you feel a bit anxious about having to give a talk in front of your class or group or when you are taking part in a play or a school assembly.

The next bit of the magician's book tells you all about how we communicate with each other.

There is much more to communicating than just talking and a *lot* of beautiful sapphires to collect while you learn all about it!

1. All about how we talk

When you talk you use different parts of your mouth and throat to make speech sounds. Sounds go together to make words and words can go together to make sentences.

Everyone sounds different when they talk because we all have different shaped mouths and throats and we move our speech muscles in slightly different ways. See if you can find out the names of some of the parts of the body that we use when we speak.

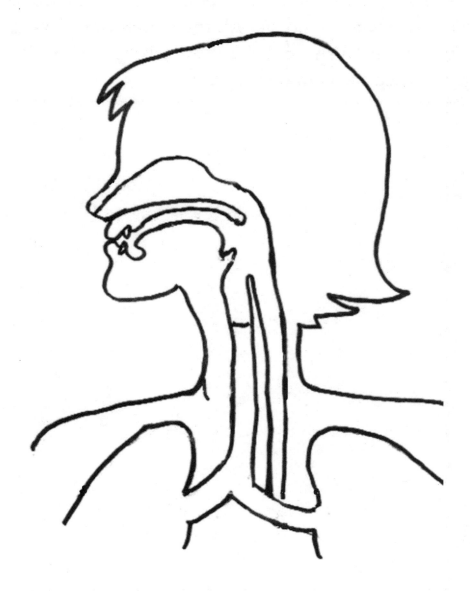

2. Conversations

What does the word 'conversation' mean?

_____

_____

Draw a picture or write about a conversation you have had today. Who were you talking with? Who started the conversation? What was the conversation about? Who did the most talking? Who did the most listening? How did the conversation end?

3. Talking skills

When we talk to each other we do lots of different things that help to make what we say clear and easy to understand.

Let's imagine…

Imagine that you are watching television. You are watching a programme about the two friends, Simon and Jenny. They are having a conversation about the day they went on a school trip together. What are they doing when they talk to each other? Where are they looking? How do they sound? Do they both talk at the same time?

See if you can fill the speech bubble with lots of words to describe good talking skills.

4. Listening skills

Do you think that listening is the same as hearing?

Imagine that you are walking in a busy town with someone in your family. Draw or write all the things that you imagine yourself hearing.

Now put a circle around the things you would actually *listen* to. Can you listen to more than one thing at the same time?

5. Let's imagine

Mike and Bill.

Mike and Bill are best friends. **Bill** is very good at talking to other people but **Mike** makes lots of mistakes. See if you can spot all the mistakes that Mike makes in this story.

One day Mike was mending his skateboard outside his house when Bill walked by. Mike heard Bill's footsteps and looked up. Bill waved and said, 'Hi Mike!' Mike looked back at his skateboard and carried on trying to fix the wheel.

'What are you doing?' asked Bill, kneeling down beside Mike.

'My dad gave it to me,' said Mike. 'I think he's at work.'

'It's a great looking skateboard,' said Bill. 'How did the wheel come off?'

Mike didn't answer so Bill carried on talking.

'I used to have a skateboard but it broke when my brother tried to race it down a steep hill and it crashed into a tree at the bottom. I was really fed up and…'

'Sally isn't at home so that means we can have fish pie for tea,' Mike said suddenly.

Bill pulled a face. He wrinkled his nose and curled his lips as though he'd tasted something really disgusting. 'Oh I *love* fish pie,' he said.

'Do you?' asked Mike, not looking up.

'No, 'course not…can't stand it!' replied Bill. 'And anyway, what's fish pie got to do with Sally?'

But Mike had fixed the wheel on his skateboard and was ready to try it out. 'Bye then,' called Bill. 'See you at school tomorrow.'

'I wonder if Bill's got that new computer game yet,' thought Mike as he raced down the path on his board.

Let's imagine (continued)

How many mistakes did you spot? Write them here.

6. Taking turns

What do we mean when we talk about 'taking turns'?

_____

_____

Why is it important to take turns when we talk to each other?

_____

_____

What would happen if we didn't take turns when we talked to each other? Imagine yourself having a conversation with some friends. Imagine that they are talking so much that you don't get a chance to say anything. What do you feel? What happens? What would you like to do?

_____

_____

_____

_____

7. Looking

Why is it important to look at each other when we are talking?

_____

_____

Who does the most looking? Is it the person who is speaking or the person who is listening?

_____

_____

Imagine what it feels like when the person you are talking to isn't looking at you.

_____

_____

Imagine that you are talking to your friends and you are looking down at the floor. Imagine what your friends might be thinking.

_____

_____

8. Keeping good eye contact

If people are able to look at each other easily when they are talking and listening it is called 'keeping good eye contact'.

Lots of people find this very difficult to do, especially if they are feeling a bit shy.

Keeping good eye contact is an important part of feeling and looking confident. So now you're going to put your imagination to work by thinking up some games for practising eye contact.

Draw or write about your games here.

9. Body talk

Sometimes it is possible to know how someone is feeling even before they say anything.

They *show* us how they feel by the way they are standing or sitting and by the expression on their face.

What do you think the person in this picture is feeling?

Let's imagine...

Close your eyes and imagine someone who you know. What does this person look like when they are happy?... How do they stand?... Do you think they would be moving their hands or would they be still?... What would their face be like?

Make as clear a picture as possible in your mind.

Now imagine what this person would look like if they were nervous...

What about if they were sad?...

How would they look if they were surprised?

When you are ready, see if you can draw or write about some of the things that happen when we use our bodies to talk.

10. How do we sound when we talk?

People talk in lots of different ways. Some people talk very quickly. Some people talk quite slowly. Some people have a high voice and some talk with a very low, deep-sounding voice. Perhaps you've heard people talking in a different language to yours or with a different accent?

Now and then we all have difficulty getting our words out. Write the words 'My cat is black and white' in the speech bubbles and show what different speech mistakes can sound like.

We might mix our words up by mistake. What do you think that might sound like?

We might use different sounds for the one we meant to say:

Lots of people repeat sounds or words by mistake:

All these different ways of talking can happen to all of us a little bit and to some of us a lot.

11. Speaking in a group

Talking to just one person some-times feels different from talking in a group.

Let's think about this a bit more.

Let's imagine...

Imagine that you are with some friends and you are telling them about something that you did yesterday. Where do you imagine yourself being? How do you feel?

Now imagine giving a talk to your whole class. Does that feel different or the same?

Imagine that your talk has finished and it went really well. What did your classmates do that helped it to go well? What did *you* do? Write about some of the feelings.

It's hard to speak in a group when

_____

_____

It's easy to speak in a group when

_____

_____

12. What I feel about speaking in a group

If I were going to speak in a group it would be OK if

_____

_____

_____

_____

_____

It would be difficult for me if

_____

_____

_____

_____

13. Talking time

Are there times when you feel that it's difficult for you to say what you want to say? Let's think of some times when it's easy to talk to each other and some times when it's not so easy.

It's easy to talk when

_____

_____

_____

_____

It's harder to talk when

_____

_____

_____

_____

14. What I like about the way I talk

Think about your own talking now. Think about all the things that you do when you talk, as well as how you sound.

Imagine that you have just had a long conversation with a friend. Write a list of all the things that you did to help the conversation to go well.

I imagined that I was talking to _____

This is what I did to help the conversation to go well:

_____

_____

_____

_____

_____

_____

15. The magic mirror

Think about what you have found out while you have been collecting sapphires.

Look in the magic mirror. What do you see?

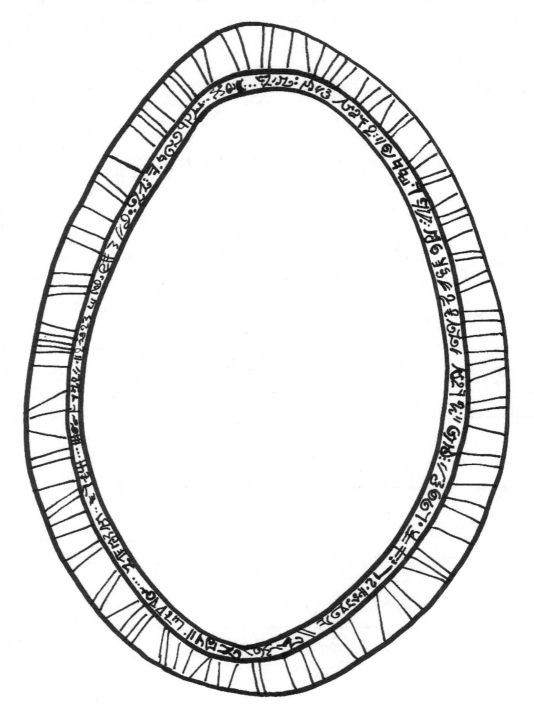

RAINBOWS

Solving Problems

Keep those sapphires safe while we hunt for rainbows!

As you learn new things you get better and better at solving problems. For example, maybe you wouldn't know how to untangle a knot in your shoelaces unless you knew how to tie a knot in the first place.

Problems to be solved come in all shapes and sizes.

Sometimes we have little problems to solve (like untying knots) and sometimes we have bigger problems (like what to do if our best friend doesn't want to play with us).

Sometimes we have problems that just seem too huge for us to solve on our own.

So, next we're going to look at how we can help ourselves to solve problems.

1. Let's imagine

Imagine if problems were animals or plants or anything at all that could be drawn. What would they be?

Fill this page up with drawings that somehow show us what little problems and medium-sized problems and really big problems are like.

2a. A problem shared

Choose one of your 'problem' pictures and give it a name. For example 'friend problem' or 'homework problem' or 'maths problem'.

Let's imagine...

Look at what you have drawn and imagine yourself becoming the image – just to see what that would be like.

When you pretend that you are this image, what does that feel like?... Do you feel big and strong, or small and not very strong at all?...

What colour are you?...

If you can move, how do you move?...

Problems like to be solved! As this problem, what would you like to happen now?...

When you are ready, step out of being your image problem and go back to being you again...

Was the problem the size you expected it to be? What did you find out?

Draw your problem again now that you know a bit more about it.

2b. Problem talk

If you could talk to your image problem now what would you want to say to it?… What does it say back to you?… Imagine yourself having a conversation with it…

Do you want to ask it to do anything?

When you are ready, draw or write about what happened.

2c. Where has it gone?

Now imagine the *opposite* of the problem you chose. What does this look like? Imagine its colour, how it feels to touch, its size and weight.

Draw the opposite of your problem image here.

2d. Something changes

Now draw a third picture. Fill the whole page with a picture that somehow shows us a solution (an answer) to your problem.

2e. Making it happen

How can you help this change to happen
in real life? What is the first small thing
that you could do that would help?

If I want to solve this problem I could

_____

_____

_____

_____

_____

_____

_____

Imagine that!

3. One less problem

Think of a time when you solved a problem on your own. Draw or write about it here.

4. Still puzzled?

Sometimes we meet problems that we just don't understand at all. It's as if the problem came from another planet!

Think about what you need to do if you come across something that you don't understand or that you need help with.

If I don't understand something I could

_____

_____

_____

_____

_____

_____

_____

5. A bit of magical wisdom

Let's imagine... THE BOOK OF WISDOM!

Imagine that you have a special book. A book that knows the answer to lots of different questions. It is especially good at solving problems.

When you talk to this book it always listens and sooner or later it always comes up with an answer.

If you have a question or a problem to solve write or draw about it here.

Close your eyes and imagine that you can ask the Book of Wisdom to help you. What does it tell you? Write or draw what it says.

Sometimes, the answer doesn't come straight away. Sometimes you have to wait a few days and then – just when you least expect it, you'll find the answer!

6. The magic mirror

What have you found out about yourself while you searched for rainbows?

Look in the magic mirror. What do you see?

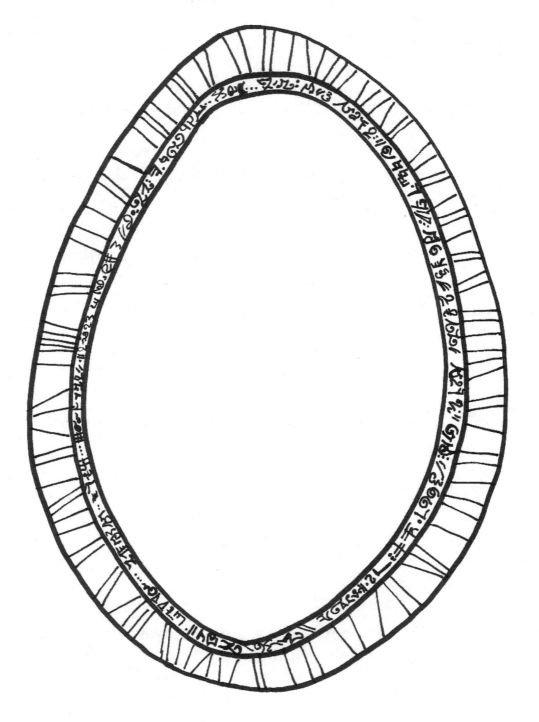

VIII

MOONBEAMS

Setting Goals

You have almost finished collecting treasure. While you've been drawing and writing and imagining, you've also learnt lots about yourself and other people.

Now all that's needed is for you to take some time to set some goals for yourself. You can think of these as 'targets' – things that you would like to achieve in the future.

We know that the people who have most fun in life and who feel good about themselves are the ones who set themselves small targets every so often.

Sometimes they set themselves big targets as well!

It's up to you what you want to achieve for yourself.

In these last few pages I'd like you to imagine that you are collecting moonbeams while you go on a journey into space.

1a. Taking off

Let's imagine...

Let's imagine that you can travel into the future in your own special space ship. What sort of a space ship is it?... Is there room for two people inside or just enough for one?... Imagine that you can step into the space ship...

Have a look at the controls. There are lots of them. There's a button that has a sign under it saying 'To the stars'. When you're ready to go all you have to do is press this button and the space ship will gently take off and head up into the sky. Ready?...

Your space ship takes you through the clouds... The sky around you is becoming a deeper and deeper blue and you can see the stars shining ahead of you... You're going high in to the place where everything and anything is possible...

Somewhere up here is your own special star and the space ship is going to take you right up close to it so you can see it really well...

Notice all the little details about this very special star as the space ship hovers near it and circles around it...

If there is something you have to get done or a goal you want to set for yourself then this is the star that will be able to show you what it will be like for you once you've achieved it.

When you are ready, draw your star on a large sheet of paper.

1b. Just the right star

When you have drawn your star, close your eyes again…and imagine that you are back in your space ship…

Imagine that there is a beam of light shining out from your star into the sky. It can project pictures on to the sky as though you were at the cinema.

As you watch you can see a big screen forming in the sky ahead of you. Onto this screen walks a person…it's you! This is you after you've achieved your goal.

What do you look like on the screen?… What is the 'future you' doing?… What did you do to make this happen?… What did you need to have or to know so that you could achieve your goal?… How is 'you' on the screen different from you sitting in the space ship?…

The future you says goodbye and is walking away now… As you watch, the beam of light from the star starts to get fainter and the screen starts to fade until eventually it has disappeared all together…

Time now to leave the stars. Take one last look around… Press the button that says 'home' and away goes the space ship, through the deep blue sky…through the floating clouds…slowly and gently back down to the ground…

As you get out of the space ship notice if you feel any different now to how you felt when you first set off… Are you ready to come back to the room now?… Let the images fade away… Have a stretch and open your eyes…

2. A letter to myself

Take some time to write a special letter to yourself from the future, telling yourself how to work on your goal.

_____

_____

_____

_____

_____

_____

_____

_____

3. Footsteps

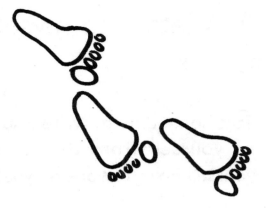

One thing I'd like to be able to do is

_____

_____

These are the steps I need to take

_____

_____

_____

_____

_____

_____

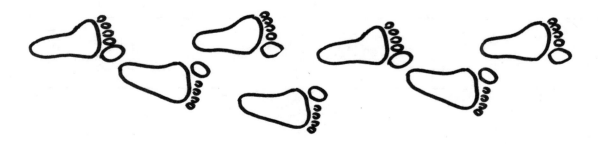

4. If I were famous

I would like to be famous for

5. Recipe for success

I will succeed if

_____

_____

_____

_____

_____

_____

_____

6. My treasure chest

Let's imagine that your treasure chest is now full of all the wonderful things about being you.

Can you imagine the chest? What is it made of? How big is it?

Imagine that every bit of treasure somehow shows us something special about you. Each piece of treasure has a label on it to show us what it is.

It would be a shame to keep all that treasure shut away in the chest all the time, don't you think?

Imagine that every day you go to your treasure chest and take a few things out to put on show so that we can all admire them.

What treasure will you choose today?

From my treasure chest today I chose

_____

_____

_____

_____

7. Goal record sheet

My goal is

_____

_____

_____

I tried it when

_____

_____

This is what happened

_____

_____

The next thing I'm going to try is

_____

_____

8. I can change the way that I feel about myself

...by doing these things:

☐ —————————————————————————————

☐ —————————————————————————————

☐ —————————————————————————————

☐ —————————————————————————————

☐ —————————————————————————————

☐ —————————————————————————————

☐ —————————————————————————————

☐ —————————————————————————————

Put a tick in each box when you have achieved the goals that you decide on.

9. The magic mirror

Think about what you have learnt while you have been collecting moonbeams.

Look in the magic mirror. What do you see?

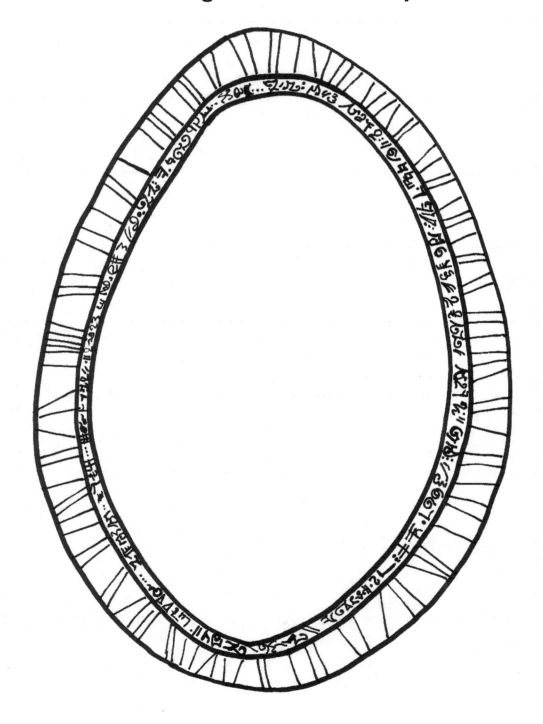

Dear Magician,

Congratulations! You have now collected all the treasure that you need for your magician's treasure chest.

Remember that it is important that you feel good about yourself no matter what difficulties you have to deal with.

Remember too that even qualified magicians make mistakes sometimes. This is all part of how we carry on learning about ourselves and about other people.

You have used your imagination to learn all sorts of things already and you know that imagination is free and it's always there for you!

Now that you have this magician's power, use it wisely and have fun with it.

With very best wishes,

Deborah

(Magician's Assistant)

Part Four

Working with Parents

Introduction

This part of the book offers a guide for discussion and suggested activities for working with parents who are supporting a child with low self-esteem.

The underlying philosophy

There are three key principles which inform the structure of this approach:

1. Self-esteem is a 'family affair'. It is much easier to support an individual with low self-esteem where there is already healthy family esteem, but where this is tenuous, the two aspects can be nurtured alongside each other. Parental and sibling feelings of self-worth and competence should be kept in focus throughout. Where grandparents are key figures in a child's life, their involvement should also be encouraged.

2. Changes in interaction patterns will be most effective where parents are able to reflect on the relevance of these to their family life and, through reflection, have some understanding of the nature of change, what might make change difficult and what helps to make change more manageable.

3. Supporting healthy self-esteem is 'a way of being' and not something we do to someone else to 'make them feel better' (see p.18).

Naturally, there is no such thing as an 'ideal course' since families and children differ so much and because self-esteem is not something that can be parcelled up and 'gifted' to a family by professionals! Also very naturally, the strategies we use will depend largely on our professional training and on the reasons that might bring a group of parents together for a course such as this. The suggestions therefore allow for flexibility in content and in the way that each session is delivered.

As with the children's activities, the ideas presented in this section of the book have mainly arisen from discussions with numerous parents, children and adult clients during my work as a therapist over a period of more than 20 years. In all that time I think that two of the biggest lessons that I learnt were to listen a great deal more than I talked and to ask limited questions that would invite parents and children to reflect on their interactions rather than to swamp them with advice. The giving of information (as opposed to advice) is a different matter: knowing the facts helps us to make informed decisions. With this in mind, each session therefore includes facilitator-led explanations and aims to enhance awareness, give parents the opportunity to discuss and try out a variety of specific activities, and encourage reflection on the impact of any changes made.

There are ten central topics to be covered in eight sessions of approximately two hours' duration. This format could also easily be adapted for use on a more intensively structured course. Although this would not then allow time for all the observations and gradual assimilation of ideas into daily life, support could be offered in the form of review sessions where resources permit. The ideas could also be used with individual families.

Whichever way you decide to use the material, it is recommended that you cover all the themes to some degree so that parents have a full understanding of the foundation elements of self-esteem and of the part that adults play in supporting healthy self-esteem in children.

I also strongly recommend that you incorporate some of the children's imagework activities into the sessions. These could be used during warm-ups or to illustrate points raised during discussions. Once parents feel comfortable enough with each other in the group, actually doing the imagery exercises is a powerful way of demonstrating the usefulness of this approach.

Further information for the suggested discussion points can be found in Part One (theoretical background) and in the facilitator's notes for the children's activities (Part Two).

Working with groups

When I first qualified as a speech and language therapist I was faced with the daunting task of co-facilitating an adult therapy group without any real knowledge of group processes. I was lucky to have a good mentor but, looking back on it now, I realise just how much I took for granted about the way that groups function, about adult learning and about my role as facilitator. Things move on! The psychology of groups is now an accepted part of most training courses for health professionals at both undergraduate and post-graduate levels. However, this is an important starting point for a section on working with parents and so here is a reminder about some of the main areas for consideration.

Groups offer the opportunity for:

- pooling resources and ideas
- reducing the facilitator's 'teacher'/'magician' status
- encouraging self-help and self-evaluation
- active engagement in the learning process

- spontaneity and creativity as participants discuss ideas with more than one person
- experience of positive feedback and support from other parents.

But…groups can also:

- foster dependence on group support
- be more challenging for some group members than for others
- tempt facilitators into giving more advice than they would if working one-to-one.

So…as facilitators we need to:

- continually reflect on our own skills and learning
- understand how adult group interactions differ from one-to-one therapy/teaching
- be clear about our own role within the group.

Reflective practice

To state a rather obvious fact – every group is different and can be challenging to practitioners in different ways. Much of our learning as group facilitators happens as a result of reflecting on sessions and making adjustments as we go along, but if you haven't run a group before my message is don't be hard on yourself – do try and enlist the help of a co-facilitator and do try and observe one or two sessions of an established group if at all possible. It is very difficult to run an adult group of this sort on your own and notice or remember everything that happens. It can be exhausting and does not make reflective practice an easy task.

At the end of each session, or as soon as is feasible, take time to think about the content, pace and 'flow' of the meeting; the interactions betweens parents; and your role as facilitator. Note the successful elements and any modifications you would want to make for future meetings of this group or for future courses.

Throughout these sessions we are also encouraging parents to be reflective and self-aware. To begin with some parents may feel that this is quite contrived and unnatural and that it has negative effects on their natural way of interacting with their child. If this is the case then your own experience of reflective practice may help to clarify this approach. Being self-aware in this context is about taking time to think about what we say and do – it is about being fully conscious or 'mindful' of how our interactions affect others.

Group interactions

Parent groups can be extremely supportive of individual members and are often a highly effective way of working. Sharing ideas and experiences can help to alleviate the burden of complex feelings such as anxiety, guilt, loss or sadness that almost inevitably surface when parents start to think about how they interact with their children and about their own levels of self-esteem. If parents feel OK about themselves they are much more likely to be supportive, congruent, accepting and nurturing to their children. In fact, many weary and stressed parents would undoubtedly benefit from attending a self-esteem course just for themselves. Increased healthy self-esteem in their children would surely be a naturally resulting outcome of such an approach.

Groups also hold a variety of different associations for people, not all of them positive. Coming to a group may initially heighten unwanted feelings of dependency (on the group and on the facilitator). Some parents may have had unpleasant experiences of social or family groups. Some may have memories of very formal learning at school and may feel uncomfortable about speaking in a large gathering or may expect to be 'told what to do'. The ethos of the group should therefore be explained right at the start (or preferably in discussions with each family before the first session).

At the first group meeting parents will need to spend time getting to know each other and should be given the opportunity to speak briefly to as many other group members as possible. This may take up to 20 or 30 minutes of the session but it is worth doing in order to foster an atmosphere where each person feels comfortable about making contributions in larger group discussions. It can also help to prevent situations such as a very verbal parent unwittingly dominating the first session or a quieter parent feeling disappointed that he or she didn't have the opportunity to talk about his or her child. Subsequent sessions could start with small groups or pairs doing an exercise based on one of the activity sheets used with the children.

There is specific time set aside during each session for reflecting on the previous week so these initial warm-ups are simply a way of orientating the group and, after the first week, need to be kept very brief.

Once a group is under way there is generally a natural shift in how individuals come together for particular tasks. You may find that you have two smaller groups, one of which is very talkative and takes twice as long over any of the discussions as the other, quieter group. This is where two facilitators can be particularly useful – one for each group – so that timings are kept more or less equal. In the long run this can prove more successful than trying to mix people up to get a more even balance, since individuals may feel far less comfortable in these contrived groups.

The role of the facilitator

Whereas in one-to-one interactions we can structure discussions around subjects which have particular significance for the family we are working with, there may be some discussions in a group which don't immediately seem applicable for everyone. A primary task for the facilitator is therefore to help parents to reflect on the relevance of each session to their own family life and to feel comfortable in voicing any concerns that they may have.

Familiar issues are bound to recur in most groups: issues of behaviour management are a particular favourite. You may question how much or how little you want to be involved in such discussions according to your professional orientation but they often prove to be a vital part of the success or failure of self-esteem interventions. You may want to consider inviting an outside speaker to run a session purely around this theme.

The following guidelines are a selection from *Helping Adolescents and Adults to Build Self-Esteem* (Plummer 2004) and are based on experience and on ideas from various sources, including Michael Jacobs' book *Swift to Hear: Facilitating Skills in Listening and Responding* (Jacobs 1992, pp.89–107).

- Help the group to stay on track when they are working in pairs and in larger group work but avoid being prescriptive.

- Aim to promote communication between group members as often as possible. Participants should be encouraged to direct their questions and comments directly to each other with the facilitator keeping things moving.

- Do not underestimate or devalue your own abilities. Offer your knowledge as a 'resource' for the group. Occasional self-disclosure of feelings and thoughts can be helpful but should not be too frequent. Be honest about what you do and don't know.

- Introduce only a limited amount of new material each session. Encourage personal contributions from parents about their own experiences of using the strategies that have been discussed and tried out in the sessions.

- Aim to use a variety of materials/approaches to support different learning styles.

- Discourage lengthy problem-focused discussions and re-telling of 'how things went wrong'. Acknowledge the difficulties experienced and steer the group towards a solution-focused approach.

- Allow participants to 'discover' things for themselves.

- Respect the individual's ability to make choices even if these differ from those you might like to suggest.

- Be aware that cosy, amenable groups are not always the ones that make the most progress. Encourage creative debates!

- Look for opportunities to allow more reticent members to speak.
- Be sensitive but firm with participants who tend to dominate the group.
- Be willing for some problems to be unresolved. It is not your role to try and make everything better!
- If a group member says something crucial right at the end of a session acknowledge the importance but be clear that you are not able to discuss it at that point. For example: 'This is a big issue and it deserves a lot of time, not just the few minutes we can give it now. Let's be sure to talk about it next time.'
- And finally, think about your own self-esteem and how best to support this.

References

Jacobs, M. (1992) *Swift to Hear: Facilitating Skills in Listening and Responding.* London: SPCK.

Plummer, D. (2004) *Helping Adolescents and Adults to Build Self-Esteem.* London: Jessica Kingsley Publishers.

Suggestion for further reading

Houston, G. (1990) *The Red Book of Groups.* London: The Rochester Foundation.

Getting Started

Aims of this session

- to give an overview of the course
- to begin to establish group support
- to offer some basic information about how self-esteem develops
- to begin the exploration of personal elements of self-esteem

Suggested format

1. Introductory/warm-up activity (see p.224)

2. Facilitator-led explanations:

   * Introductions and 'housekeeping' information (fire drill, tea and coffee-making facilities etc.)
   * Overview and philosophy of the course
   * What is healthy self-esteem? (Information Sheet 1A)

3. Possible discussion points:

   * Parental feelings and expectations (Activity Sheet 1.1)
   * What are the benefits of healthy self-esteem?
   * What raises your self-esteem? What lowers your self-esteem?
   * Does your child have different levels of self-esteem according to situation/task?
   * What raises/lowers your child's self-esteem?
   * The iceberg of self-esteem (Activity Sheet 1.2)

4. Closing activity:

   * Volunteers share one insight gained during the session

5. At home:

   * Complete a self-esteem checklist (Activity Sheet 1.3) OR
   * Observe child in different situations (at home, with friends, while out) and look for indications of healthy self-esteem

Facilitator notes

What is healthy self-esteem? (Information Sheet 1A)

See Part One, Chapter 2, pp.21–23.

This information sheet can form the basis for a discussion about how we build different areas of self-esteem in our lives (instead of thinking of self-esteem only in terms of a global sense of self-worth and competency).

It is also important at this point to acknowledge the skills and understanding that parents bring to these discussions. The starting point should always be that parents are (or have the potential to be) the experts on their own child.

Discussion points

FEELINGS AND EXPECTATIONS (ACTIVITY SHEET 1.1)

To be completed and discussed in pairs. Common themes could be shared with the whole group to help people to recognise that they have similar worries or expectations.

This is a chance for parents to clarify for themselves what it is that they are hoping to gain from the course both personally and for their child. One of the questions you could pose to get things going is 'If you could only ask two questions during this entire course what would they be?'

WHAT ARE THE BENEFITS OF HEALTHY SELF-ESTEEM?

Start this off with a group brainstorm.

If it has not already been discussed this would be a good opportunity to talk about having 'healthy' levels of self-esteem rather than necessarily thinking in terms of 'high' levels of self-esteem (p.18–19).

WHAT RAISES YOUR SELF-ESTEEM? WHAT LOWERS YOUR SELF-ESTEEM?

Beginning with an exploration of personal self-esteem may well bring up parent–child relationship issues and perhaps feelings of guilt or concern about parenting skills. It is less likely to provoke anxiety if this discussion takes place in small groups of two or three. The general 'themes' can then be brought back to the main group and summarised briefly.

DOES YOUR CHILD HAVE DIFFERENT LEVELS OF SELF-ESTEEM ACCORDING TO SITUATION/ TASK?

Relate this to Information Sheet 1A

Possible areas for discussion might be:

- relationships with friends
- relationships with family
- at school (academically)
- meeting new people

- doing things independently
- when being creative
- in sports.

WHAT RAISES/LOWERS YOUR CHILD'S SELF-ESTEEM?

The emphasis of this discussion should be on strategies for raising self-esteem which parents are already aware of or have already found to be successful with their child.

Factors which lower self-esteem might include such things as:

- making mistakes
- when something new occurs
- illness
- difficulties with friends
- being 'blamed'.

Factors which raise self-esteem (taken from a selection of ideas from several parent and teacher groups):

- learning a new skill
- spending individual time with a parent
- being asked for his/her opinion
- being praised/encouraged
- having experience of solving problems
- seeing that it's normal to feel anxious sometimes
- being prepared for changes
- being with someone who 'knows the ropes'
- doing something they love
- having things explained to them clearly
- realistic expectations from others
- seeing that it's OK to make mistakes.

THE ICEBERG OF SELF-ESTEEM (ACTIVITY SHEET 1.2)

See children's activity sheets PEARLS 2, 3 and 4 and SAPPHIRES 9.

Low self-esteem can be viewed in terms of an iceberg. There are some indications of low self-esteem that can be heard and seen. These overt aspects are equivalent to the part of an iceberg that lies above the water.

When someone is coping with any sort of difficulty there are usually many aspects which either lie below the surface of their conscious awareness or are not apparent to other people. These covert aspects may include physical feelings as well as the thoughts and emotions involved.

Of course, many of the covert aspects of a difficulty will be displayed overtly, although not necessarily in a way that might be expected. For example, embarrassment may 'appear' in the form of verbal aggression. Supporting children with low self-esteem will involve exploring and helping them to modify elements of both parts of the iceberg.

Brainstorm this as a whole group. Each parent then selects the relevant elements for their child's personal iceberg. This is also a self-help tool for a later date. As some aspects are reduced or eliminated there will be a knock-on effect on others so the iceberg can be redrawn. Parents can then compare the different versions of their child's iceberg at different stages.

See Appendix A for a compilation of observations and reported feelings made by several groups of primary school teachers when asked to identify signs of low self-esteem in children in their classes.

Facilitate a group discussion about how little or how much we reveal our emotions and thoughts through our actions and body language. Children will generally have a more limited range of 'feeling' words according to their age and experience. Talk about the possibility that adults who have experienced similar circumstances may assume more 'adult' feelings in children than they are actually capable of. In contrast it is also possible that we can underestimate the depth of feeling experienced by some children just because they don't yet have the vocabulary to describe them.

Closing activity

Insights could be around the following:

- What I understand about self-esteem.
- What I understand about my child's self-esteem.

At home activity: Self-esteem checklist (Activity sheet 1.3)

The boxes can be shaded to the degree in which each statement is thought to be true. For example, 'very true' would mean the whole box is shaded, 'quite true' would mean perhaps just a small part of the box being shaded, 'not true at all' would obviously mean no shading. This checklist could be revisited at various stages to help parents to review their child's progress. Relate this task to the concept of domain-specific self-evaluations, developmental appropriateness and the natural fluctuations that occur according to circumstance, mood etc.

Information sheet 1A

Global and specific self-esteem

Home + School + Social life + Society

↓

Personal relationships   Personal experiences

Interpretation

↓

Self-concept

↓

Self-evaluation

↓

Self-esteem in specific areas of life

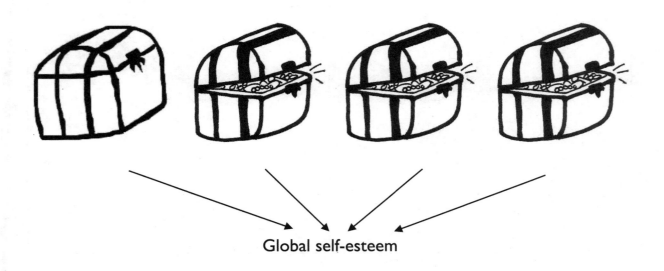

Global self-esteem

231

Activity 1.1

Feelings and expectations

What are your feelings as you start the course? What do you feel confident about?	What are your expectations of this course? What would you like to know more about?
What would you like your family to have achieved by the end of this course?	What do you feel are the main obstacles that you and your child will need to overcome?

Activity 1.2

The iceberg of low self-esteem

OVERT

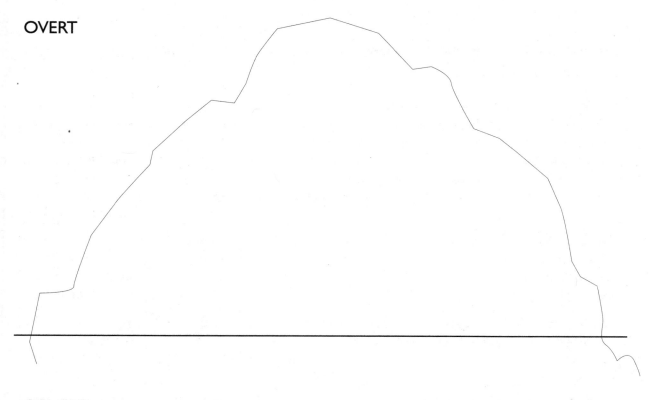

COVERT

Activity 1.3

Self-esteem checklist

Shade in the boxes to indicate how much each of these statements is true for your child for most of the time.

copes well with new or difficult situations/tasks	talks positively (and realistically) about own abilities e.g. 'I can do this', 'I'm good at this'	mixes well with other children of own age (doesn't boss, bully or tease others)	can be assertive in saying 'no' to peers when this is appropriate	shows a variety of emotions and copes well with more 'difficult' emotions such as anger and sadness
talks positively about peers without putting self down	concentrates well	can tolerate making mistakes	is at ease meeting new children	is willing to ask questions if doesn't under- stand something
takes pride in own appearance	will persevere with difficult tasks	can tolerate some degree of frustra- tion without giving up on things	can play with others co-operatively	volunteers for activities at school (e.g. school play)
is self-motivated	is realistic when comparing self to others e.g. under- stands that older siblings may be more adept at a task because of age or experience	is able to work in- dependently at school or ask for appropriate help when needed	can engage in negotiations over family rules where appropriate	can tolerate being given 'constructive feedback'
has lots of energy for trying new things	accepts praise	demonstrates creative thinking	is comfortable talking with known adults	recognises own successes
copes successfully with setbacks (e.g. not being picked for a team)	talks positively about own attrib- utes e.g. 'That was hard but I was really determined'	respects differ- ences in others	enjoys being involved in making decisions	believes that he or she is a likeable person
can cope with a degree of self- responsibility appropriate for age	enjoys school and gets excited about learning new ideas or skills	demonstrates an appropriate range of social skills for age	does not con- stantly dwell on past difficulties	is willing to talk about worries and difficult feelings

Foundation Element: Self-Knowledge

Children's Section: Who Am I? (RUBIES)

Aims of this session

- to strengthen group support
- to introduce the first foundation element of self-esteem
- to introduce the use of imagery as a way to explore personal patterns of thinking and feeling

Suggested format

1. Brief warm-up activity (see p.234)

2. General feedback about personal checklists completed at home (Activity Sheet 1.3)

3. Facilitator-led explanations:

   * What is self-knowledge? (Information Sheet 2A)

4. Possible discussion points:

   * Introduction of communication guidelines (Activity Sheet 2.1)
   * How do we define who we are?
   * Complete child's 'life path' and discuss with one other person (Activity Sheet 2.2)
   * What makes my child unique? How is he or she similar to other family members?
   * How can I help my child to understand his or her family history?

5. Closing activity:

   * Volunteers share one insight gained during the session

6.   At home:

* Complete a character sketch for your child (RUBIES Activity Sheet 6 p.115) or all the family draw self-portraits together

Facilitator notes

Feedback on personal checklists (Activity Sheet 1.3)

Look for themes, similarities and differences. Was this difficult/easy to do? Did the exercise help to clarify any points or bring particular behaviours to the attention of parents? Were there any surprises?

What is self-knowledge? (Information Sheet 2A)

The box 'ways for my child to explore self-knowledge' can be completed as ideas occur throughout the session. This is also suggested as a specific discussion point.

Discussion points

INTRODUCTION OF COMMUNICATION GUIDELINES (ACTIVITY SHEET 2.1)

See also discussion of confidence groups (pp.44–47).

Talk about the meaning of each guideline and the possible effects on self-esteem when they are forgotten. Encourage parents to think of three or four specific examples of how they have used each one in the past and/or could use them in the future. We cannot of course be completely consciously aware of all these things all the time – we would probably be exhausted by the effort before the end of the day! These are simply guidelines and the more that people try them out the more they become second nature.

- *Staying aware of body language* – Being aware of our body language enables us to ensure that *what* we are saying matches *how* we are saying it. For this to be sincere, we need to be aware of our own feelings and attitude and remain true to them. Carl Rogers (1961) suggested that congruency engenders a sense of trust in the other person because they feel that they are with someone who is genuine. It also means being aware of how children will read our posture, facial expression and gestures. For example, wherever possible it helps the communication process if we can be on the same level as our child (not towering above them, asserting our authority!).

- *Listening fully* – This refers to listening fully to your child and looking for the message behind his words and behaviour to help you to understand what he is thinking or feeling. Sometimes our own anxieties, thoughts, feelings and preconceptions can get in the way of listening accurately to someone else. This is very normal but children need plenty of experiences of really being heard and confirmation that their thoughts and opinions are valued and their feelings are acknowledged and understood.

- *Using 'I' not 'you'* – This is often a difficult task but it is a helpful pattern to establish within families. Discuss the way in which we sometimes appear to hand over responsibility for how we feel to children. A statement such as 'You make me so angry' assumes a very different locus of control to 'I feel angry about what you just said/did'. Similarly, 'I am very proud of you' has a different feel to it as compared to 'You make me very happy'.

- *Giving constructive feedback* – See notes for STARS Activity Sheet 3 and GOLD Activity Sheet 1. This should include discussion about describing behaviour, not labelling the child, and also about sharing positive feelings with children: 'I love walking home with you after school', 'I really like reading stories with you', 'I really enjoy being with you' etc.

- *Looking for the common goal* – There will inevitably be times when a parent and child have a common goal but very different ideas about how to get there. Sometimes reminding ourselves of this can help us to find a compromise or help us to allow a child to make her own decision without imposing our version of what we would do in that situation.

- *Using language that children understand* – Talk about 'matching' children's language levels. Every interaction need not be a teaching opportunity. Use words that children understand. Try using images or ask your child to tell you how she *imagines* things to be (see Part One, Chapter 1).

HOW DO WE DEFINE WHO WE ARE?

See Part One, Chapter 2 and notes for RUBIES Activity Sheets 2, 8 and 12.

COMPLETE CHILD'S 'LIFE PATH' AND DISCUSS WITH ONE OTHER PERSON (ACTIVITY SHEET 2.2)

The life path can be drawn metaphorically or with sketches to represent actual events. So 'starting school' might be represented by a drawing of a school building or by a mountain (it was tough going) or a sun (he loved it from the first day).

This activity can highlight many different vulnerabilities and strengths and plenty of time should be given for sharing in pairs and for bringing together any important themes in the large group. This should therefore be done early on in the session or reserved for one-to-one discussion with parents.

WHAT MAKES MY CHILD UNIQUE? HOW IS HE OR SHE SIMILAR TO OTHER FAMILY MEMBERS?

See notes for RUBIES Activity Sheets 7, 8 and 13.

Who does your child 'hang out' with? Why do you think this is? Does he prefer adult company/younger children/being alone?

This may be an appropriate point to discuss sibling relationships. Unfortunately, siblings can often feel very left out when one member of the family is the focus of attention because of a particular difficulty. Reinforce the idea that, throughout these sessions, everything covered relates to a 'whole-family approach' not just the individual child with low self-esteem.

HOW CAN I HELP MY CHILD TO UNDERSTAND HIS OR HER FAMILY HISTORY?

Brainstorm this and complete the box on Information Sheet 2A.

Some ideas might be:

- through games
- make a scrapbook or photo album together
- have an 'interview with granny'
- find out two new pieces of information about a family member.

Look at results of the brainstorm. Choose at least two ideas from the list that appeal to you as a family that you will try at home.

Closing activity

Insights might be around themes such as:

- My child's position in the family.
- Exploration of family history.

At home activity

Each parent chooses to complete a written character sketch of their child (see p.117) or to draw self-portraits. Remind parents to keep feedback to their child positive and descriptive during the drawing of self-portraits together.

Reference

Rogers, C.R. (1961) *On Becoming a Person: A Therapist's View of Psychotherapy.* London: Constable.

Suggestion for further reading

Faber, A. and Mazlish, E. (1982) *How to Talk So Kids Will Listen and Listen So Kids Will Talk.* New York: Avon.

Information sheet 2A

Who am I?

Foundation element: Self-knowledge

Children love to hear and to tell stories about themselves. Familiar themes might be 'Tell me the story about when I was born', 'What happened when I had to go to hospital when I was a baby?', 'Do you remember when I got that prize/got bullied/fell over/climbed the tree…?' Even when parents have related the same story on several different occasions there is often still a need to hear it many more times! This is a major way in which we learn about ourselves – by repeatedly hearing and telling our stories.

A strong sense of 'self' and a sense of 'belonging' are vital elements of healthy self-esteem. It is important for children to know something about their family history as well (parents, grandparents etc.).

Ways for my child to explore self-knowledge

Activity 2.1

Communication guidelines

These guidelines are important for all communications and will be useful to keep in mind during interactions with your child.

- Staying aware of body language

- Listening fully

- Using 'I' not 'you'

- Giving constructive feedback

- Looking for the common goal

- Using language that children understand

Activity 2.2

My child's life path so far

Imagine that you could represent your child's life as a path that he or she has travelled along from birth to the present day. Imagine what this path looks like. Is it smooth or does it have 'rocky' patches? Are there bridges? Ravines? Lakes? Woods? Crossroads? Take some time to draw your child's life path, marking on it any important events. As you draw this, think about how these events might have affected the way that your child felt physically, mentally and emotionally at all the different stages.

Foundation Elements: Self and Others and Self-Awareness

Children's Section: Friends and Feelings (SILVER)

Aims of this session

- to introduce the second and seventh foundation elements of self-esteem
- to expand on communication skills and guidelines
- to explore the link between thoughts, emotions and behaviour
- to share ideas about how to help children to understand their emotions

Suggested format

1. Brief warm-up activity

2. Feedback on character sketches and self-portraits

3. Facilitator-led explanations:

    * Ways for adults to support healthy self-esteem in children (Information Sheet 3A)

4. Possible discussion points:

    * What happens when our own self-esteem is 'hooked'?
    * The validity of our emotions and patterns of emotional expression (Activity Sheet 3.1)
    * Making requests, not demands
    * Saying 'no' when your child makes an unreasonable request
    * Giving constructive feedback to your child
    * Giving and receiving praise
    * Helpful interactions (Information Sheet 3B)
    * Self-awareness (Information Sheet 3C)

5. Closing activity:

  * Volunteers share one insight gained during session OR
  * Discuss a goal for the week with one other person

6. At home:

  * Make general observations of family ratios of demand/praise/request/negative feedback speech

Facilitator notes

How we see ourselves will affect how we view others. If a child thinks that people are judging her then she is likely to act in a defensive way. This could mean that she becomes aggressive or perhaps very passive. If she fears rejection she may be tempted to avoid forming close relationships altogether. Her own behaviour will then undoubtedly affect how others behave towards her.

This cycle of feelings and behaviour within relationships is not inevitable. When a child has healthy self-esteem she will tend to trust others more and will be more discerning in her choice of friends. In turn, she will undoubtedly attract genuine respect and liking from others.

Feedback on character sketches and self-portraits

See notes for RUBIES Activity Sheet 6.

How did the activity go? What do you think your child/you gained from this? Did you enjoy it? Were there any surprises? How does your version (of the character sketch) compare to your child's own version?

Ways for adults to support healthy self-esteem in children (Information Sheet 3A)

See also communication guidelines on pp.236–237.

Briefly discuss each point, asking for examples. Are there any other aspects that parents would like to add?

Discussion points

WHAT HAPPENS WHEN OUR OWN SELF-ESTEEM IS 'HOOKED'?

Family therapist Virginia Satir identified four common communication patterns when self-esteem is threatened:

> Whenever there was any stress, over and over again I observed four ways people had of handling it. These four patterns occurred only when one was reacting to stress *and at the same time* felt his self-esteem was involved. (Satir 1972, p.59)

The four patterns of communication are placating, blaming, computing and distracting. All these are non-assertive communication patterns.

- *Placater* – doesn't want to 'rock the boat' or upset anyone in any way so will tend to agree with everything and try to make everyone happy. Takes the blame for everything, apologises frequently.

- *Blamer* – finds fault with everything and blames everyone else for whatever goes wrong; will use phrases like 'Why do you always…' and 'You never do…' The blamer is aiming to appear 'strong' when actually they are feeling low in self-worth.

- *Computer* – cool, calm and collected. Tends to use long words in order to sound as though she really knows what she is talking about. Will often refer to something she has read on the subject. Appears 'without emotion', quite detached and very still (no expressive hand gestures!).

- *Distracter* – whatever the distracter does or says is irrelevant to whatever else is going on because he feels out of place. He is constantly moving around and fidgeting. He asks questions or makes comments that have nothing to do with the topic being discussed.

Discuss specific examples of these patterns in both adults and children. Discuss how adults have choices about how we act but young children are more limited in their reaction patterns. We need to understand the message behind the behaviour and acknowledge the feeling. We may not always get this right of course, so it is also important to encourage children to *tell* us if we are wrong in our guesses: 'No, I don't feel awkward, I'm angry about_____'.

SELF-AWARENESS (INFORMATION SHEET 3C)

Being self-aware involves being able to identify our emotions and understand the reasons why we feel and behave the way we do in different situations. It also involves being aware of all our senses and of the way in which our thoughts can affect us physically. Self-awareness is the cornerstone of realistic self-evaluation.

Facilitate a discussion about the different states of awareness that we can be in – fully aware, daydreaming, 'fantasising', on 'automatic pilot', sleeping, under hypnosis, focused entirely on one thing. Different states of awareness are appropriate at different times and to be self-aware all the time would probably be impossible in normal daily life (and probably make us impossible to live with!). However, we cannot self-evaluate effectively unless we have basic skills in this foundation element.

THE VALIDITY OF OUR EMOTIONS AND PATTERNS OF EMOTIONAL EXPRESSION (ACTIVITY SHEET 3.1)

See notes for SILVER Activity Sheets 3, 4, 5 and 6.

Once again, exploring this on a personal level can engender insights and ideas in relation to how children express and experience emotions. This could lead on to a discussion about how behaviour patterns might persist, even when the consequences are unpleasant for us. This activity could also be facilitated in terms of emotions and behaviours purely in relation to parent and child interactions. For example:

- *Emotion*: Love.

- *How I normally express it*: Ask for/give a hug.

- *What I experience as a consequence*: My child pulls away from me and I feel rejected.

MAKING REQUESTS, NOT DEMANDS

Some parents may find imaginary scenarios a useful way to assimilate concepts. Try the following:

> Shelley, a very competent and creative mother, has designed and constructed a colourful game to help Rebecca learn how to produce the sound 's'. She sits opposite Rebecca (who is four-and-a-half years old) at a low table. They begin to play the game. While playing, Rebecca is constantly swinging one leg and either kicking the table leg or kicking her mum in the process. Shelley's response is to repeatedly tell Rebecca to 'Stop doing that'. Rebecca stops momentarily but starts to swing her leg again as soon as it is her turn in the game. Shelley becomes more and more agitated and eventually 'threatens' to end the game if Rebecca doesn't sit still.

What are some of the possible feelings (for both Shelley and Rebecca) behind this interaction? What are some of the alternatives for a successful interaction that will support self-esteem?

Some strategies to think about:

- Be aware of your body language in relation to your child. Stay at his or her level.

- Decide what you would like the outcome to be but be prepared to negotiate if this is appropriate.

- Use 'I' statements. Take responsibility for how you are feeling.

- Be clear about the separateness between you and your child. Just because he or she says or does one thing doesn't mean that you have to react in a certain way.

- Be specific in your requests; encourage your child to be specific too.

- Acknowledge your child's point of view and feelings (empathise).

- Keep an eye on your common goals.

- Avoid allowing your self-esteem to be 'hooked'.

Modelling ways of making reasonable requests will help children learn to be assertive and reasonable rather than aggressive and demanding.

SAYING 'NO' WHEN YOUR CHILD MAKES AN UNREASONABLE REQUEST

Notice your immediate physical reaction to the request. Your body will let you know whether or not you feel your child is really being unreasonable or you are just not feeling up to the request at this moment.

Be consistent. If you usually say 'no' to this particular request *and have reasonable, valid reasons for this* then try not to be tempted to give in on some occasions because you are tired or so that you can have a 'quiet life'. Children need to feel secure in knowing what your expectations are.

Use the same guidelines as for making requests, not demands.

Tell your child 'no' and give a clear, uncomplicated reason as to *why* you are saying 'no'.

Check that your body language is also saying 'no' without looking or sounding aggressive.

GIVING CONSTRUCTIVE FEEDBACK TO YOUR CHILD FOR EXAMPLE, WHEN HIS OR HER BEHAVIOUR HAS BEEN INAPPROPRIATE

Appropriate feedback is non-judgemental, clear information to your child about how his or her behaviour affects you or has affected someone else. For example 'I feel cross when you do that because_____' or 'Nathan was very upset when you ignored him because _____'.

Wherever possible, talk with your child about the behaviour that would have been more acceptable. Praise the desired behaviour as soon as you notice it.

GIVING AND RECEIVING PRAISE

See notes for STARS Activity Sheet 3.

It is important for us to feel comfortable giving feedback to each other and to our children in the form of appropriate praise and compliments. It is easy to reject compliments that have been given in all sincerity by responding with such things as 'Oh, it was nothing'; 'I wouldn't be able to do it like that again'; 'I just grabbed the first thing out of the wardrobe'. If compliments and praise are given genuinely and received openly they can act as extra 'coinage' in our self-esteem pots!

- How do you feel when you are praised?
- What is an assertive way of accepting praise?
- How do you praise yourself?
- How do you praise your child?

Closing activity

Insights shared could be around themes such as family interaction patterns or giving constructive feedback.

Reference

Satir, V. (1972) *Peoplemaking.* London: Souvenir Press.

Information sheet 3A

Ways for adults to support healthy self-esteem in children

giving time

loving

trusting

listening

having realistic expectations

encouraging friendships

describing actions
(not labelling behaviour)

accepting

making positive requests
(defining the appropriate behaviour)

acknowledging
feelings

noticing small
triumphs

respecting

rewarding

playing

providing
security

encouraging

celebrating achievements

negotiating

modelling appropriate behaviour

giving appropriate responsibility

empathising

shared problem-solving

sharing stories/special time together

defining appropriate boundaries

giving unqualified praise

Information sheet 3B

Helpful interactions

Helpful	Unhelpful
Praise is undiluted e.g. 'Well done for putting away your toys'	Qualifying praise by adding negatives e.g. 'Well done for putting away your toys. Why can't you always do that?'
Giving non-verbal signs of approval e.g. thumbs up, smile, wink etc.	Only giving attention when there is a 'problem'
What you say matches *how* you say it	Using ambiguous or complicated praise e.g. 'It's sometimes really nice for me to see you play quietly'
Noticing small achievements and commenting positively. Explaining *how* you know your child has done something well e.g. 'I can see that you have taken great care to put all your toys in the right places'	• Only commenting on big achievements • Being vague about why you are praising e.g. 'good girl'
• Describing desired behaviour accurately and concisely • Being prepared to admit your own mistakes and to apologise	• Using 'labels' such as 'shy', 'clumsy' • Being vague or too general about desired behaviour e.g. 'Be good', 'Behave'
Making expectations and tasks clear, explicit and manageable	Criticising with no information about how or what to do to improve e.g. 'You're hopeless, you're always forgetting your homework book'
Encouraging self-evaluation e.g. 'What did you do that helped you to remember your homework book?'	Setting unrealistic or vague targets e.g. 'You need to remember everything your teacher tells you'
Encouraging and using 'I' statements e.g. 'I felt so proud of you when you helped Josh'	Using 'you' statements e.g. 'You make me so angry sometimes'
Seeing behaviour as communication. Looking for the feeling behind the action	Taking comments or behaviour personally e.g. 'You're always showing me up'
Acknowledging the child's feelings e.g. 'You're upset at the moment'	Denying or making light of child's feelings e.g. 'Don't be silly, it's nothing to cry about'
Being clear and consistent about boundaries and rules	• Being over-protective or over-critical • Being inflexible about rules that are no longer useful

Information sheet 3B

Helpful Interactions (continued)

Helpful	Unhelpful
Collaborating with your child to come up with imaginative problem-solving strategies	• Telling your child what to do • Making the problem out to be unimportant e.g. 'It's easy to ask your teacher questions. You just need to put your hand up more often'
Acknowledging your child's wish even though it can't be fulfilled in reality e.g. 'Wouldn't it be wonderful if I had two pairs of hands so I could carry the shopping and hold your hand at the same time? What else could we do if we had two pairs of hands?'	Being overly practical and 'realistic' all the time e.g. 'I can't hug you now, I don't have two pairs of hands!'
Being honest and clear about your requests e.g. 'I need you to put your coat and gloves on now because the bus leaves in five minutes'	Being vague or failing to explain your aims e.g. 'Get ready now!'
• Using non-judgemental words like 'difficult' and 'easy' • Using positives e.g. 'Walk slowly'	• Using judgemental words like 'good' and 'terrible' • Using negatives e.g. 'Don't run'

Information sheet 3C

All my senses

Foundation element: Self-awareness

Self-awareness involves being able to identify our emotions and understand the reasons why we feel the way we do in different situations. It also involves an awareness of the way in which our thoughts can affect us physically.

In order to be constructively self-aware children need to be able to concentrate and focus on what their senses are telling them, noting changes and recognising that they have some control over the way that they feel and behave.

Which sense do you think you use the most? When you close your eyes for a while do you hear sounds that you hadn't noticed before (such as the clock ticking)?

Ways for my child to develop positive self-awareness

Activity 3.1

Patterns of emotional expression

Think about how you normally express your emotions and consider whether or not your responses are always useful/ appropriate.

Emotion	How I normally express this emotion	What I experience as a consequence

Is there anything from your list that you would like to change and could realistically alter at this stage? Look on this as an experiment. How could you alter a particular way that you express or experience an emotion? What do you anticipate would be the result of this change?

Session 4

Foundation Element: Self-Acceptance

Children's Section: Feeling OK about Being Me (GOLD)

Aims of this session

- to introduce the third foundation element of self-esteem
- to think about parent modelling in more depth
- to explore concepts of learning, achievement and making mistakes
- to further explore the link between thoughts, feelings and actions

Suggested format

1. Brief warm-up activity

2. General feedback on interaction patterns at home

3. Facilitator-led explanation:

   * Self-acceptance (Information Sheet 4A)

4. Possible discussion points:

   * Family patterns
   * Modelling that it's OK to make mistakes
   * The school system and your child
   * Common patterns of self-talk that lower self-esteem (Activity Sheet 4.1)
   * Completing an 'asset' jigsaw (Activity Sheet 4.2)
   * What is confidence?

5. Closing activity:

   * Volunteers share one insight gained during session OR
   * Discuss a goal for the week with one other person

6. At home:

   * Experiment with increasing praise

   * Spend five minutes three times during the week consciously listening to your child with full attention and enjoyment

Facilitator notes

General feedback on interaction patterns at home

What did you notice? Did this precipitate any changes? What do you feel really good about with regard to interactions at home?

Self-acceptance (Information Sheet 4A)

See Part One, Chapter 2.

As discussed in the introductory chapters to this book, our self-concept includes all aspects of how we see ourselves and self-acceptance therefore also includes body awareness and feeling OK about our physical appearance.

Discussion points

FAMILY PATTERNS

Discuss the relative importance given to academic/social/creative achievements within the family. This could be facilitated as a discussion in pairs or threes with time given for brief feedback in the main group on any common themes.

MODELLING THAT IT'S OK TO MAKE MISTAKES

See notes for GOLD Activity Sheet 3.

Do you feel comfortable telling your child when you have made a mistake or apologising if you get something wrong/misunderstand him? How do you apologise? Be specific. Try to avoid saying things like: 'I'm sorry, I'm a hopeless mum/dad.' Labelling yourself in this way gives a negative message to children about how they should evaluate themselves.

THE SCHOOL SYSTEM AND YOUR CHILD

What do you feel affects your child's self-esteem at school? Focus on positive aspects as well as exploring any negatives.

COMMON PATTERNS OF SELF-TALK THAT LOWER SELF-ESTEEM (ACTIVITY SHEET 4.1)

See Part One, Chapter 2.

Explore the following patterns of negative self-talk and collect some examples of each. Link this to the discussion points for Session 3 and the idea of modelling positive self-talk for children.

Self-talk patterns	Examples
I know what you think (otherwise known as mind-reading!)	you obviously think I don't know what I'm doing
total disaster (catastrophising difficult events)	my whole world will fall apart if I don't know anyone at the party
these things always go together (If 'a' happens then 'b' ALWAYS follows)	if I volunteer for a part in the school play I will forget my lines – I always do
everyone and always (overgeneralising)	everyone always thinks I'm stupid
compared to you	I can never match up to my brother/sister/anyone else
I should (it is an unwritten law from somewhere)	I will feel guilty/will somehow be punished if I don't do this/feel this
I must	I don't have any choices. This is the only option
the whole of me	I am so useless – my teacher didn't even say good morning to me
the world says/does	everyone knows that…if you lose things you're stupid
I blame the cat	the cat/teacher/neighbour makes me feel stupid
vaguely speaking	it's all Terry's fault

COMPLETING AN 'ASSET' JIGSAW ACTIVITY SHEET 4.2

It may be difficult for some children to appreciate the skills that they have or to see the relevance of these skills in different areas of their lives. Parents can help them to draw on these 'assets' in a variety of situations.

In order to complete the jigsaw, each person thinks of at least three things that their child enjoys doing. They then think about what skill or personality trait (asset) their child has that enables them to enjoy this pastime. Each asset is entered in the jigsaw. Discuss how many of these could be used when tackling a problem in a different area of life.

This could also be done as a parental asset jigsaw: what skills do you have in other areas of your life that you bring to parenting?

Finish the exercise by encouraging parents to appreciate their child's and/or their own greatest achievements. Emphasise that these are personal achievements, not achievements compared to anyone else.

WHAT IS CONFIDENCE?

See notes for GOLD Activity Sheet 6.

Closing activity

Insights could be around the themes of:

- What I understand about self-acceptance.
- What I understand about my child's patterns of thinking.

Information sheet 4A

Feeling OK about being me
Foundation element: Self-acceptance

Recognising our achievements and being able to accept sincere praise and compliments is an important aspect of self-acceptance. This element also involves recognising the areas that we can change or are already working on and those things that it would be much more difficult to change or may even be impossible to change.

Part of self-acceptance involves understanding the difference between making mistakes and failing. Young children are often not aware that older children and adults make mistakes too and that this can be a very productive way of learning – some of the most inspired inventors and scientists achieve their best creations through making mistakes in design and learning from them!

Ways for my child to explore self-acceptance

Activity 4.1

Some common patterns of self-talk that lower self-esteem

I know what you think

these things always go together

total disaster

everyone and always

compared to you

vaguely speaking

I should/I must

the world says

the whole of me

I blame the cat

Activity 4.2

My child's asset jigsaw

What would you most like other people to know about your child? What do you appreciate about him or her? What are his or her skills and assets?

Complete the 'asset jigsaw'.

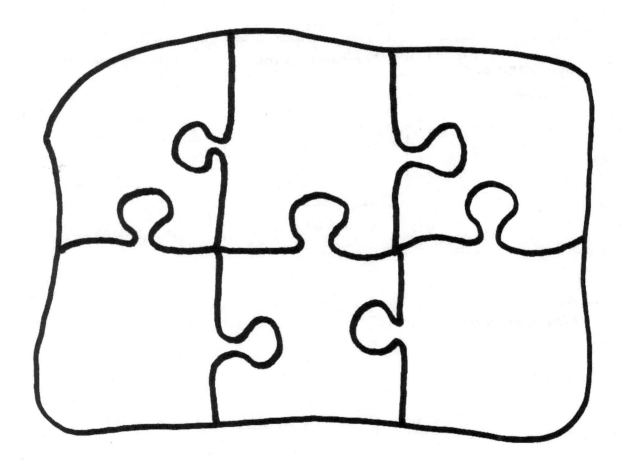

Session 5

Foundation Element: Self-Reliance

Children's Section: Taking Care of Myself (PEARLS)

Aims of this session

- to introduce the fourth foundation element of self-esteem
- to explore personal and family stress management
- to share ideas about helping children with their worries

Suggested format

1. Brief warm-up activity

2. General feedback on praising and listening tasks

3. Facilitator-led explanations

    * Self-reliance (Information Sheet 5A)

4. Possible discussion points

    * Sharing ideas for relaxation and stress reduction
    * How does stress affect your child?
    * Dealing with worries
    * Short relaxation (Activity Sheet 5.1)

5. Closing activity

    * Volunteers share one insight gained during session OR
    * Discuss a goal for the week with one other person

6. At home:

    * Include your child in planning and carrying out a fun activity together that involves being out of the house
    * Choose one activity from the children's section and ask children to 'teach' parents how to do it

Facilitator notes

General feedback on praising and listening tasks

What happened? How did you structure this? Did your child praise you? What were your feelings about these activities?

Self-reliance (Information Sheet 5A)

See Part One, Chapter 2.

Discussion points

SHARING IDEAS FOR RELAXATION AND STRESS REDUCTION

See notes for PEARLS Activity Sheets 5, 7, 8 and 9.

What works for you? What doesn't work? Do you give yourself time for specific periods of relaxation or a few moments to yourself? Include ideas for relaxing physically *and* mentally.

HOW DOES STRESS AFFECT YOUR CHILD?

What physical, mental and emotional effects have you noted? What works to relieve these? Is there a family pattern in how your child reacts/copes with stressful situations?

DEALING WITH WORRIES

See notes for PEARLS Activity Sheets 10, 11 and 12.

Spend some time sharing resources for 'worry' stories and other ideas which parents have found to work (including self-help methods for adults).

SHORT RELAXATION (ACTIVITY SHEET 5.1)

See notes for PEARLS Activity Sheet 4.

This is the adult version of the exercise in Appendix B.

Parents will probably know each other well enough by this stage in the course to feel comfortable doing this relaxation in the whole group. Experiencing the exercise for themselves will also help them to see the relevance of some form of tension-awareness exercise for their child.

Closing activity

Insights could be around the themes of:

- What I understand about being self-reliant and the management of stress.
- What I understand about my own management of stress.
- What I understand about my child's patterns of stress management.

Information sheet 5A

Taking care of myself
Foundation element: Self-reliance

Of course, the skills needed to build self-reliance are acquired very gradually in childhood but each step can be a tremendous boost to self-esteem, especially if they are noted and celebrated.

A child's physical achievements such as being able to dress himself or ride a bike are often acknowledged and celebrated but there are other areas of self-reliance which may be missed by both the child and by adults as well. These small triumphs of emotional self-care can be a powerful force for increased motivation, independent thinking, self-efficacy and emotional resilience. We need to be on the look-out for them and encourage them just as much as the physical signs of self-reliance.

When children start to develop a degree of self-reliance they are more able to enjoy the exciting and fun things in life and more ready to cope with things that are challenging or difficult.

Ways for my child to explore self-reliance

Activity 5.1

Relaxation

This type of relaxation involves directing your attention to different areas of your body and just being aware of any sensations. By keeping your attention on physical sensations you can be focused in the 'here and now' rather than caught up with thoughts about the future or the past. By observing your body in this way you will also probably find that you naturally allow any areas of tension to relax and release.

You may want to make your own recording of this exercise. If you do, remember to read the instructions very slowly and calmly with plenty of pauses to allow yourself time to focus fully.

Settle yourself into a comfortable position and allow your eyes to gently close, withdrawing your attention from the outside world. Begin to notice your breathing – without trying to change anything, just noticing the natural pattern as you breathe in and out. You might notice this by being aware of the rise and fall of your stomach or you might be aware of the feel of the air as you breathe in and out through your nose.

Continue to focus on your breathing for a few moments. When other thoughts come into your mind, just acknowledge them and go back to being aware of your breathing…

Now take your attention to your feet. Focus on your feet as though you had never really thought about them before. Notice the sensations in your feet just at this moment. They may feel warm or cool, numb or tingling, painful, tense, relaxed. There is no right or wrong feeling. Whatever is there just notice it.

Now allow your attention to leave your feet and move easily and smoothly to the lower part of your legs. Notice whatever feeling is there just at this moment… Now move up to your knees and the upper half of your legs and notice whatever feeling is there… Now to your hips and lower back…and then gradually along the length of your spine… Begin to notice your shoulders, focus on all the feelings around your shoulders. Notice the back of your shoulders, across the top of your shoulders and down into your arms…

Feel what's happening in your arms… Whatever is there, just notice it… Remember there are no right or wrong feelings. Whatever you can feel is OK…

Activity 5.1

Relaxation (continued)

And now focus on your hands and fingers... Notice the backs of your hands...the palms of your hands...and each of your fingers in turn...

Now the lower half of the front of your body... Move your attention along the front of your body until you reach your chest...and go a little deeper and see if you can notice your heart beat... Again, as other thoughts enter your mind, just let them pass through and refocus your attention back to your body... Now to your shoulders again. Be fully aware of your shoulders... Then becoming aware of your neck – the sides of your neck, the back of your neck... Be aware of the sensations in and around your throat...

Become aware of your jaw now. Are your teeth pressed together or are they slightly apart so that your jaw is relaxed?... Notice your eyes and the sensations around your eyes... Become aware of your forehead and notice any expression on your face... Moving your attention now to the top of your head...down the back of your head...and resting once again at your shoulders...

Now, instead of thinking of yourself in parts, be aware of your whole body...sensing your whole body...being aware of how sensations change from moment to moment... Continue to focus in this way for a few moments.

Now, while still sensing your body, start to listen to whatever sounds there are around you... Begin to move your hands and feet a little bit... In a moment you will open your eyes. When you do, focus your gaze on one particular thing in the room and, while you look at it, keep sensing your body and listening to the sounds around you... So, when you feel ready, open your eyes and look at one thing with your full concentration. Now shift your gaze to something else...and come back to the room fully, allowing other thoughts to return. You may want to stretch or shift your position.

Foundation Elements: Self-Expression and Self-Confidence

Children's Sections: More Than Just Talking (SAPPHIRES) and Solving Problems (RAINBOWS)

Aims of this session

- to introduce the fifth and sixth foundation elements of self-esteem
- to explore ways of helping children to develop important social skills
- to share ideas about helping children to express themselves fully
- to explore different ways of tackling family and individual 'problems'
- to share ideas about how to help children to develop their confidence

Suggested format

1. Brief warm-up activity

2. General feedback on outdoor activity planning and 'teaching' activity

3. Facilitator-led explanations:

    * Self-expression (Information Sheet 6A)
    * Self-confidence (Information Sheet 6B)

4. Possible discussion points:

    * What are social skills?
    * Ideas for promoting social skills
    * Exploration of familiar and unfamiliar ways of solving problems

5. Closing activity:

    * Volunteers share one insight gained during session OR
    * Discuss goals for the week with one other person OR
    * Group members discuss possible goals for each other

6.   At home:

   *   Choose one problem-solving method with which to explore a family dilemma/problem together (with full involvement of your child)

Facilitator notes

General feedback on outdoor activity planning and 'teaching' activity

Did your child enjoy being involved in planning activities, making choices, being the 'teacher'? How are choices incorporated into your family life?

Facilitate a general discussion about the importance of children being allowed to make choices. This is especially valuable at times of major changes, such as starting a new school or moving house, when they could perhaps be involved in choosing a theme for their bedroom or helping to choose school items etc.

Self-expression (Information Sheet 6A)

The box can be completed as ideas occur during the session. Talk about the many different ways that we communicate with each other. Discuss the patterns of communication that parents have noted in their children. Explore themes of developmental progress and family patterns. Talk about how children need to be given the opportunity to communicate. This involves giving space and time and really listening to them (not talking *at* them all the time or asking them lots of questions with very little time for them to answer). Talk about congruence – checking that our body language matches our words and our true feelings. Understanding non-verbal communication can be particularly difficult for children if the significant people in their lives are ambiguous in their messages of affection and chastisement.

Refer back to the communication guidelines discussed in Session 2.

Self-confidence (Information Sheet 6B)

Ask for parents' ideas about what constitutes self-confidence and how they see this element in relation to themselves and how they see it manifested in others.

Discussion points

WHAT ARE SOCIAL SKILLS?

IDEAS FOR PROMOTING SOCIAL SKILLS

See notes for all SAPPHIRES activity sheets.

Discuss SAPPHIRES Activity Sheet 5 (pp.181–182). I have sometimes given this as a 'do at home' activity for the children and parents to share. This has often engendered useful family discussions about expectations of communication ability and levels of understanding about social skills – some children simply don't understand or have never learnt these skills.

EXPLORATION OF FAMILIAR AND UNFAMILIAR WAYS OF SOLVING PROBLEMS

The same method of problem-solving may not necessarily work for different situations and different types of problem. This is why it is important to develop creativity in dealing with difficulties.

Problem-solving is about focusing on possible solutions rather than dwelling on the problem itself. Discuss times when parents have solved or reduced a problem. What did they do? How did they arrive at a solution? What steps did they take? Encourage parents to be as precise as possible in recalling the details of this and to think about their thought processes, feelings and actions. What worked? What didn't work? What did they learn from the experience?

Try giving small groups of parents different problems to solve and then ask them what skills they needed in order to solve them. A group of teenagers given this task came up with the following very comprehensive list:

- experimental skills
- quick thinking/lateral thinking
- making yourself clear to others
- willingness to contribute your own ideas
- confidence in your own opinion
- coping with disappointment
- not getting angry/frustrated
- thinking positive thoughts and trying your best
- it's OK to make mistakes
- put all the ideas together to make a better idea.

Closing activity

Insights shared could be around the themes of:

- What I understand about social skills.
- What I understand about the way that I express myself with my child.
- What I understand about creative problem-solving.
- What I understand about my child's methods of problem-solving.

Information Sheet 6A

More than just talking
Foundation element: Self-expression

This element is about with how we communicate with each other through our body language, facial expression and tone of voice as well as the words we use.

Learning to 'read' other people's non-verbal communication is a skill which some children have difficulty in mastering.

Self-expression is also about recognising and celebrating the unique ways in which we each express who we are.

Ways to help my child explore self-expression

Information Sheet 6B

Solving problems
Foundation element: Self-confidence

Self-confidence involves developing our knowledge and abilities so that we feel able to experiment with different methods of problem-solving and can be flexible enough to alter what we are doing if needed.

We all have creative potential but many of us fail to use it constructively. The amount of creativity we use is closely related to our self-concept.

As children learn to tolerate the frustration of making mistakes and begin to experience success, so they start to trust in their own judgements and decisions more and more. This helps to confirm their abilities and self-worth and gives them confidence to know that they will be able to cope with future difficulties effectively.

Each time they solve a problem this gives them experience of having more choice in what they do. Choice leads to a feeling of control and to higher self-esteem.

Ways to help my child explore self-confidence

Make-believe, Playing Games and Telling Stories

Aims of this session

- to explore the role of play in building self-esteem
- to explore the importance of sharing stories

Suggested format

1. Brief warm-up activity

2. General feedback on outcome of problem-solving activity

3. Facilitator-led explanations:

   * The importance of play in child development and self-esteem (Information Sheet 7A)

4. Possible discussion points:

   * How competitive and co-operative games can affect self-esteem
   * Rough and tumble play and construction skills
   * Commercially available stories
   * Stories made up by parents
   * Stories about real events in a child's life

5. Closing activity:

   * Volunteers share one insight gained during session OR
   * Discuss a goal for the week with one other person OR
   * Group members discuss possible goals for each other OR
   * Group members take turns to say one thing they have learned during the session and how they will put it into practice during the coming week

6. At home:

   * Play one game of child's choice for at least 20 minutes

     * Choose one of the recommended self-esteem stories to read together or for your child to read and then tell you about it

Facilitator notes

General feedback on outcome of problem-solving activity

What method did you use? How did this work? What was the outcome? What were you pleased with? Would you try the same method again?

The importance of play in child development and self-esteem (Information Sheet 7A)

This does not need to be an in-depth presentation on the psychology of play! However, discussion about family experiences of play can quickly highlight how children learn different skills throughout their early years, including language skills, problem-solving, understanding cause and effect, construction skills, dexterity and many more. Start with any recollections that parents may have of play when their children were babies (e.g. peek-a-boo) and how this type of play gives children the experience of taking turns and initiating an interaction. Talk about the development of imaginary play. Can parents remember at what age their children started to act out imaginary scenarios? What do they think their child was learning through this process?

Discussion points

HOW COMPETITIVE AND CO-OPERATIVE GAMES CAN AFFECT SELF-ESTEEM

Whilst there is certainly a place and a need for competitive games and sports in our culture, young children, especially those who already have low self-esteem, can find these very daunting. In order to be able to cope successfully with competition they need to develop a certain amount of emotional resilience and an understanding of the rules of competitive games. Sometimes such rules are too complex for young children and losing to an older sibling or a peer becomes yet another confirmation of their feelings of lack of competence or lack of control

Co-operative games, on the other hand, can be a pleasurable way of supporting self-esteem for both parents and children. Sharing a game together where no one is a winner or a loser can strengthen bonds of affection and inject a crucial element of humour into the process.

Facilitate a discussion about the use of games at home. This might include active games, board games, word-games, computer games, etc. What are parents' experiences of playing games with their children? Share ideas for fun games to play with different age groups.

Talk specifically about humour as a great boost to self-esteem. Discuss the differences between humour and sarcasm or 'gentle teasing' which may undermine a child's feelings of self-worth.

ROUGH AND TUMBLE PLAY AND CONSTRUCTION SKILLS

Does your child enjoy this type of play? What skills do you think she learns through this play? Can she cope with rough and tumble play without crossing the line into aggression? What about construction play? Is this a good way for your child to 'unwind' or does she get easily frustrated when something doesn't work? What skills does she learn through construction play? How can you support her in this without doing it for her?

COMMERCIALLY AVAILABLE STORIES

Throughout childhood (and, in fact, throughout life) the building and maintenance of healthy self-esteem is intimately linked with our 'imaginative' abilities. Storytelling, in all its many forms, provides an important means of fostering this link. Through stories, children have the opportunity to *imagine* life; to begin to understand that what we *think* affects the way that we experience and influence our environment and the events and relationships that we encounter.

What are parents' experiences of reading/being read to as a child? Parents who do not read may be concerned that their children are missing out on this aspect when it is discussed in the group, but 'made-up' stories can be a very rewarding way of encouraging a child's imaginative abilities and many children obviously also enjoy telling parents about the books that they have read at school or by themselves.

Take time to share resources, including practical information about libraries etc. if this is appropriate.

STORIES MADE UP BY PARENTS

See above. Discuss how we tell stories all the time when we tell our family, friends or colleagues about something that has happened or something we have seen on TV or read about. It is not such a big leap from this to telling stories to children about made-up events and characters. These stories don't even have to be particularly elaborate or lengthy.

STORIES ABOUT REAL EVENTS IN A CHILD'S LIFE

See Information Sheet 2A and accompanying notes on self-knowledge.

Closing activity

Insights could be around themes of stories or play such as:

- What I understand about my child's play.
- The importance of humour.
- A story that I've just remembered that I can tell to my child!

Information sheet 7A

Play and playing games

Play of one sort or another provides invaluable opportunities for children to experience the consequences of their actions and to experiment with different skills and different outcomes without fear of failure or of being judged unfavourably by others.

By working their imagination like a muscle children learn to problem-solve, to work through some of life's difficulties, to reach their own understanding of some of the very confusing things that happen in their world. This also helps to strengthen their emotional resilience – the ability to tolerate emotions such as frustration without being overwhelmed by them.

Ways to help my child to build self-esteem through play and through using his or her imagination

Session 8

Course Review
and Goals for the Future

Aims of this session

- to celebrate individual and family achievements
- to explore strategies for maintenance of change
- to review goals and plans for the future
- to offer information on other support facilities/information for future use

Suggested format

1. Brief warm-up activity

2. General feedback on play/storytelling activity

3. Possible discussion points:

   * Review of any changes made at home and on observed levels of children's self-esteem
   * Review of personal checklists and iceberg of self-esteem
   * How do you celebrate achievements?
   * What aspects of the course are you still experimenting with? What is your child still working on?
   * Support agencies and self-help groups
   * Helping children to cope with setbacks

4. Closing activity:

   * Group members take turns to say one or more things they now feel confident about in relation to helping their child to build self-esteem. Celebrate achievement in any way that seems most appropriate for that person.

Facilitator notes

General feedback on play/storytelling activity

How did this work? How did you feel? How did your child respond to the inter-action? Any disappointments? How would you build on or alter what you did?

Discussion points

REVIEW OF ANY CHANGES MADE AT HOME AND ON OBSERVED LEVELS OF CHILDREN'S SELF-ESTEEM

What are the biggest changes that you have made or noticed? What effects have these had? What has your child achieved? What obstacle(s) have you overcome?

REVIEW OF PERSONAL CHECKLISTS AND ICEBERG OF SELF-ESTEEM

Has anything changed? Any surprises? What are you really pleased about? What is your next step? What is the next step for your child?

HOW DO YOU CELEBRATE ACHIEVEMENTS?

Facilitate a discussion about the importance of celebrating achievements in some way and the relevance for this for children. What would be suitable ways of celebrating small achievements? This might be as simple as a smile or a 'thumbs-up' acknowledgement. What about bigger achievements? This may be an appropriate time to talk about the difference between the conditional aspect of bribery which has the potential to lower self-esteem ('If you do well I will buy you a TV for your room/let you stay up late/will be so proud of you') and the unconditional nature of celebrating with your child.

WHAT ASPECTS OF THE COURSE ARE YOU EXPERIMENTING WITH AT THE MOMENT? WHAT IS YOUR CHILD WORKING ON?

This might include discussion about things that parents would like to know more about and any objectives for the future.

SUPPORT AGENCIES AND SELF-HELP GROUPS

A chance for parents and facilitators to share ideas about available resources, possible review sessions and perhaps the idea of setting up a parent support group if there is not one already in existence.

HELPING CHILDREN TO COPE WITH SETBACKS

Natural setbacks can and do occur and it is important that children and their parents are able to ride these or problem-solve their way out of them. Talk about the strategies that parents have used in the past. Reinforce the self-help nature of the children's activities (Part Three).

Ending the group

When parent groups have been run in conjunction with a children's group it works well to co-ordinate this last session with the children's last session and then to come together for lunch and a final celebration. In groups for children who stutter this is usually the point at which children present their ideas to parents and also stage the hero's journey play mentioned in Part Two (p.95). Children then receive their certificates for individual achievements.

The iceberg of low self-esteem

fidgeting/restlessness

clingy

distracting behaviour

poor posture

switches off/has difficulty concentrating

looking away   does not complete set work or completes it hurriedly

when praised, hits out at somebody else

rarely smiles/flat expression

avoiding/withdrawing/sits by self   tearful

tongue-tied

wets self

chews nails/pen/pulls at own clothes   frequently absent from school

rocking on chair

the 'invisible' child

self-harms

likes routine   defaces own work

sets self unachievable goals

suspicious of others

restricted interactions with others/poor social skills

rough with peers/disruptive/bullies others/abusive/insults others

attention-seeking/noisy/the 'clown' of the class

frequently asks 'When is home time/break/lunch/time to go to the toilet?'

feels 'different'

feels unloved/rejected

feels misunderstood   is 'churned up' inside

angry/resentful

frustrated   depressed   intimidated   feels 'silly'

lonely/feels left out

lethargic/tired

everything is an effort

nervous/anxious/worried

frightened of failing

has stomach ache/feels sick/head aches/has dry mouth

jealous   fast heart rate

lacks control   feels inadequate/useless   feels pressured   feels hopeless

feels worthless   fearful

overwhelmed   insecure   isolated

Appendix B

Relaxation script

This type of relaxation works by focusing the mind on different areas of the body and just being aware of what that area feels like. Often, if we try to relax, we try too hard! In our efforts to relax we actually set up more tension. By observing what the body is doing there is a natural tendency simply to allow any areas of tension to relax and release. This relaxation can be done lying down or seated. Read each part very slowly and calmly with plenty of pauses to allow the children time to follow your instructions.

Sometimes if we are very anxious or nervous or tense about something it shows in our body. Our muscles become tight. Maybe they begin to ache a little bit. We might feel 'knotted up' inside. This can feel very uncomfortable. It's a really nice feeling to be able to relax your body…and it will help you to feel confident and more able to do things that are a bit difficult.

When you are ready, let your eyes close gently and settle yourself into a comfortable position.

Notice the feel of your body on the floor (in the chair)… Now start to notice your feet… Put all your attention on your feet and really notice what they feel like. Maybe they feel warm or cold; perhaps they are numb or itchy…tight or relaxed. Just notice whatever you can feel in your feet…

Now gently move your thoughts from your feet to the lower part of your legs. Let your thoughts leave your feet and just move very easily to your legs. Notice whatever feeling is there just at this moment… There are no right or wrong feelings… Whatever you can feel is OK…

Now move up to your knees…and then the top part of your legs and notice whatever feelings are there… Now start to notice your body, feel what's happening when you breathe gently in and out… Start to think about your shoulders…feel any tightness just melt away… Notice all the feelings around your neck and your head…

Let your thoughts go gently to your back…all along the length of your back…feel the relaxation spreading through your body… Thinking about your arms now. Just notice whatever is there…and down the length of your arms into your hands… Notice all your fingers one by one. Whatever is there, just notice it…

Now, instead of thinking of yourself in parts, feel your whole body relax. Just letting go…letting the floor (chair) support you and just relaxing into it… As you breathe in, breathe in relaxation…and feel it spreading through every part of

you… Breathing in…and out…like waves on a sea shore…
Lie quietly for a few moments and enjoy the feeling of being
relaxed…

(*Allow at least one or two minutes of quietness*)

Keep noticing your body and start to listen to whatever sounds
there are around you… Begin to move your hands and feet a little bit… When you
feel ready, open your eyes and look around you… Lie or sit quietly for a short while
before stretching and having a yawn…ready to slowly sit up…

Appendix C

Instructions for calm breathing exercise

Ask the children to sit in a comfortable, upright position or to lie on their backs on the floor.

Ask them to imagine that they are the yolk inside an egg and that between the yolk and the egg shell are seven other layers. As they breathe in they imagine that they are breathing along the length of the back of their bodies from their ankles to the top of their heads. They pause momentarily at the top of their heads and then as they breathe out, they breathe down the front of their bodies, sweeping under their feet. Allow plenty of time for this – at least three to four seconds for inhalation and four to five seconds for exhalation.

Repeat this six more times, but each time that they breathe they imagine a sweeping movement slightly further away from their bodies. When they reach the seventh in-breath they are sweeping a wide circle around their bodies. Inhalation and exhalation may both take longer by this stage. In a group it is best to let each child pace themselves with their breathing as undoubtedly they will all be inhaling and exhaling at different rates!

Encourage the children to take their time and to 'really let go' (without pushing!) each time that they breathe out, releasing any unwanted tension from their bodies.

When they have completed seven breaths along the fronts and backs of their bodies they repeat the process (starting close to the body) by breathing in along the right side from the feet to the top of the head and down the left side as they breathe out, moving further away from their bodies in a circle that gets bigger and bigger with each breath. Remind them to pause momentarily after breathing in each time.

This exercise also works well if the children imagine the seven colours of the rainbow as they breathe (instead of seven layers of the egg) starting with red close to the body and finishing with violet.

Appendix D

Children's books

'The House of Coloured Windows' by Margaret Mahy in *A Treasury of Stories for Eight Year Olds* chosen by Edward and Nancy Blishen (Kingfisher, 1995)

And to Think that I Saw it on Mulberry Street by Dr Seuss (HarperCollins, 1992)

Bill's New Frock by Anne Fine (Mammoth Books, 1999)

Daisy-Head Mayzie by Dr Seuss (HarperCollins Children's Books, 1996)

Dream Snatcher by Annie Dalton (Mammoth Books, 2001)

Friends and Brothers by Dick King-Smith (Mammoth Books, 1999)

Fergus the Forgetful by Margaret Ryan and Wendy Smith (Collins, 1995)

Hiding Out by Elizabeth Laird (Barn Owl Books, 2006)

Horton Hatches the Egg by Dr Seuss (HarperCollins Children's Books, 1998)

I had Trouble in Getting to Solla Sollew by Dr Seuss (HarperCollins Children's Books, 1998)

I'm Scared by Bel Mooney (Mammoth Books, 1998)

I'm Worried by Brian Moses (Wayland Publishers Ltd, 1997)

Kiss the Dust by Elizabeth Laird (Egmont Books Ltd, 2001)

Krindlekrax by Philip Ridley (Puffin Books, 2001)

Midnight Museum by Annie Dalton (Mammoth Books, 2001)

Nothing by Mick Inkpen (Hodder Children's Books, 1996)

Only a Show by Anne Fine (Puffin Books, 1998)

Scaredy Cat by Anne Fine (Mammoth Books, 1998)

Skellig by David Almond (Yearling Books, 2000)

Something Else by Kathryn Cave and Chris Riddell (Picture Puffins, 1995)

The Afterdark Princess by Annie Dalton (Mammoth Books, 2001)

The Angel of Nitshill Road by Anne Fine (Egmont Books Ltd, 2002)

The Brave Little Grork by Kathryn Cave. Illustrated by Nick Maland (Hodder Children's Books, 2002)

The Huge Bag of Worries by Virginia Ironside (Macdonald Young Books, 1998)

The Lighthouse Keeper's Lunch by Ronda and David Armitage (Scholastic Children's Books, 1994)

The Selfish Crocodile by Faustin Charles and Michael Terry (Bloomsbury Children's Books, 1999)

The Whisperer by Nick Butterworth (HarperCollins Children's Books, 2005)

Subject Index

achievement 253, 255, 274
    academic 28, 29
    personal record 42–3
    physical 70, 261
active imagination 14
activities, guidelines
    drawing 35–6
    materials for 37
    organising 35–7
Adam, praise example 66–7
adults, role 15, 18, 20, 26, 29,
    49, 221
    see also facilitators
anxiety 75, 79
awards 71
    see also Marcus; praise

behaviour therapy 16
beliefs 16
    self-limiting 28, 93
    system 63
brainstorms 36, 65
breath control 45, 78

celebrations 43, 95, 261, 274
change 16, 25, 51, 52, 54–5,
    62, 92, 94, 221
circle time 30
cognitive therapy 16
communication
    guidelines 236–7, 265
    non-verbal 32, 84, 265
    patterns 243–4
    see also interaction patterns
confidence 72–3
    see also self-confidence

confidence groups 42, 44–7
constructive feedback 237, 246
conversation skills 33, 82–6
cortisol 19, 20
Craig, 'worry box' example
    79–80

David, stuttering example 89

emotions
    emotional literacy 30
    emotional resilience 24, 61,
      261, 270, 272
    evaluating 21
    physical aspects 77
    see also feelings
empathy 20, 26, 46, 49
expansion activities 16, 30, 34,
    36, 44–7, 49, 56–8,
    68–9, 73–4, 80–1, 86–7,
    95

facilitators
    roles 223, 225–6
    see also reflective practice;
      adults
family esteem 18, 221, 224,
    238, 253
feelings 52, 60–1, 62–4, 67,
    224, 237
    developmental aspects 62,
      230
    of parents 224, 228
    somatisation 62
    see also emotions; Rachel;
      Shelley

friendships 54, 60–1, 65–8,
    243
    see also Stephanie

games 34, 270
goals
    evaluating 93
    setting 23, 28, 30, 93, 94
Greg, problem-solving example
    88
groups
    facilitating 34-35, 222–3
    gelling 34, 61, 224
    interactions 224
    rules 34, 61

hero's journey 95
humour 270

ideal self 20, 22
imagery 13, 92
    exercises 16, 36, 48, 222
    guided 15
    see also images
images 13–14, 16, 41
    and counselling 13
    exploring 16
    interpreting 14, 52
    negative patterning 15
    types 14, 41, 48
    see also imagery
imagework 14–15
imagination 14
    as creative resource 16

Author Index

Activities Index